FABULOUS
FISH
IN MINUTES

FABULOUS
FISH
IN MINUTES

QUICK AND HEALTHY INSPIRATIONS
FOR EVERY MEAL

LINDA DOESER

HERMES
HOUSE

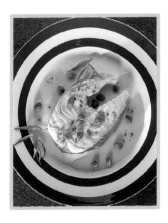

First published in 1998 by Hermes House

© Anness Publishing Limited 1998

Hermes House is an imprint of Anness Publishing Limited,
Hermes House, 88–89 Blackfriars Road, London SE1 8HA

A CIP catalogue record for this book is available from the British Library

Publisher: Joanna Lorenz
Cookery Editor: Linda Doeser
Copy Editor: Leslie Viney
Designers: Mason Linklater, Siân Keogh
Illustrator: Madeleine David

Front Cover: Lisa Tai, Designer; Tom Odulate, Photographer; Helen Trent, Stylist:
Marie-Ange Lapierre, Home Economist

Recipes: Catherine Atkinson, Alex Barker, Ruby Le Bois, Carla Capalbo, Maxine Clark, Andi Clevely,
Christine France, Carole Handslip, Sarah Gates, Shirley Gill, Norma MacMillan, Sue Maggs, Katherine
Richmond, Jenny Stacey, Liz Trigg, Hilaire Walden, Laura Washburn, Steven Wheeler
Photographers: Karl Adamson, Edward Allwright, Steve Baxter, James Duncan, John Freeman,
Michelle Garrett, Amanda Heywood, Don Last

Previously published as part of a larger compendium, *The Great Fish and Shellfish Cookbook*

Printed in Hong Kong/China

1 3 5 7 9 10 8 6 4 2

NOTES
For all recipes, quantities are given in both metric and imperial measures and, where appropriate,
measures are given in standard cups and spoons. Follow one set, but not a mixture, because they
are not interchangeable.

Standard spoon and cup measurements are level.
1 tsp = 5ml; 1 tbsp = 15ml; 1 cup = 250ml/8fl oz

Australian standard tablespoons are 20ml. Australian readers should use 3 tsp in place of 1 tbsp
for measuring small quantities of gelatine, cornflour, salt etc.

Medium eggs should be used unless otherwise stated.

CONTENTS

Introduction

Fish is the ultimate fast food – its delicate texture and flavour make it the perfect choice for preparing quick and easy meals. Most of the recipes in this book can be completed within twenty minutes and many of them take even less time.

❧

The range of fish and seafood is immense and the variety of ways in which it can be cooked is huge. Fast-cooked doesn't simply mean fried or grilled – although Pan-fried Garlic Sardines, Crumb-coated Prawns, Fish Steaks with Mustard Sauce and Grilled Green Mussels with Cumin are mouth-watering examples of these ways of cooking. Fish can also be poached, steamed, baked, deep-fried, curried and made into filling stews. It goes well with most vegetables, pasta, cheese, many herbs and spices and makes wonderful salads and delicate soups. Its versatility is almost endless.

❧

The recipes in this book are divided into four chapters. Soups & Starters includes traditional favourites, such as Clam Chowder, and some unusual appetizers, such as Sole Goujons with Lime Mayonnaise. The recipes in Fish Dishes range from Tuna and Corn Fish Cakes to Salmon with Green Peppercorns and from Sicilian Spaghetti with Sardines to Red Snapper with Coriander Salsa – something to suit all tastes. Seafood Dishes includes a traditional Thai Green Curry of Prawns, Steamed Chilli Mussels, Spicy Squid and Linguine with Clams – all of them a veritable feast made in moments. Salads similarly demonstrates the variety and versatility of fish and seafood, with recipes ranging from Warm Salmon Salad to Melon and Crab Salad and from Avocado and Smoked Fish Salad to Prawn Salad with Curry Dressing. A helpful introductory section is packed with information about types of fish and seafood, buying and storing, and a step-by-step guide to some basic techniques. Hints and tips throughout provide further advice and information.

Types of Fish and Seafood

For the purposes of cooking, fish are usually divided into freshwater and sea fish and this second group is subdivided into round and flat fish. Seafood includes edible shellfish, crustaceans, squid and octopus. Listed below are some of the most popular varieties.

Anchovy
Round fish, related to the herring family, anchovies are silvery and about 15cm/6 inches long. Fresh anchovies are not widely available. Canned anchovies are salt-cured. Whole salted anchovies are occasionally available.

Bonito
A round fish, related to the mackerel family, the silvery, striped bonito can grow as long as 90cm/ 3 feet. Fresh steaks and fillets are occasionally available, but the fish is most often sold in cans. Bonito flakes – shaved from the dried, smoked fish – are used in Japanese cuisine and are available from Asian supermarkets.

Clam
There are many varieties of this shellfish, ranging in size from 2.5–12cm/1–5 inches across. They are available fresh and bottled or canned in brine.

Cod
A round fish and the chief member of a large family that also includes haddock, hake and whiting, cod can grow to 120cm/4 feet long. It is widely available as steaks, cutlets and fillets. Whole young cod are sometimes sold. Nowadays, smoked cod is often cured and coloured, rather than smoked in the traditional manner. Both types require further cooking. Salt cod is

usually sold as fillets, but whole fish are sometimes available. It must be soaked for about 48 hours before cooking.

Crab
There are thousands of different varieties of this crustacean in a vast range of sizes and colours. Almost all have hard shells and many have a pair of large claws. Fresh crab can be bought both live and cooked. The flesh is often separated into brown meat from inside the shell, and white meat from the legs and claws. The pink coral from female crabs is regarded as a delicacy. Frozen and canned crabmeat are widely available.

Dab
A member of the flat fish family that also includes lemon sole, plaice and halibut, the rough-skinned dab ranges in weight from 225–675g/8oz–1½lb.

Dover sole
A flat fish, Dover sole is the fish used in many classic recipes. Lemon sole is quite different. The underside is white and the top surface is usually light brown. It is sold whole or in fillets.

Gurnard
A round fish, red gurnard is the most popular, but there are also yellow and grey varieties. Whole fish, weighing about 1kg/2¼lb, and steaks are available.

Haddock
A member of the cod family and also a North Atlantic fish, haddock is smaller than cod, reaching about 60cm/2 feet. It is usually sold as cutlets, steaks or fillets. Traditionally, smoked haddock is

available in fillets, which require further cooking. Finnan haddock is a whole fish soaked in brine before being smoked.

Hake
A round fish, hake grows to about 60cm/2 feet. It is mainly sold whole and as fillets. Steaks cut from large specimens are sometimes available.

Halibut

A very large flat fish, halibut is usually sold as steaks or fillets. Smoked halibut is available as a whole side or thinly sliced, and it requires no further cooking.

Herring

A round, silvery fish with a high oil content, herring grows to about 25cm/10 inches long. It is available whole and as fillets. Smoked herring, in the form of kippers, is widely available, sold whole or in fillets. It may be eaten with no further cooking, marinated, grilled or poached.

Lemon sole

A fairly large flat fish with a mottled top surface and a pale underside, lemon sole is different from Dover sole. Smaller fish are usually sold whole and larger ones are available whole and as fillets.

Mackerel

An iridescent blue-grey round fish, mackerel is usually sold whole. It weighs up to 675g/1½lb. Smoked mackerel is widely available whole or in fillets. It may be eaten without further cooking.

Monkfish

A round fish, it is rarely sold whole, not least because of its extremely ugly, large head. It is usually sold as monkfish tail, weighing 675g–1.4kg/1½–3lb. This is usually still covered with a tough, transparent membrane that must be removed before cooking or it will shrink and toughen.

Mussel

This shellfish varies considerably in size and the shells may be deep blue, black, brown or green-lipped. Live fresh mussels are widely available and they are also sold frozen and canned.

Plaice

A flat fish, it is easily distinguished by orange spots on the upper surface. It grows to about 45 cm/ 18 inches long and is sold whole or in fillets.

Prawn

This family of crustaceans ranges in size from about 5–23cm/ 2–9 inches, and in colour from blue through pink to brown. Prawns are available raw and cooked, fresh and frozen.

Red mullet

A round fish, red mullet is available in two varieties. The redder and sweeter-tasting type is sometimes known as golden mullet. It is usually sold whole.

Salmon

A round freshwater fish, salmon migrates to the sea to feed before returning to rivers to spawn. Fresh salmon is usually the Atlantic variety and it may be sold whole, in steaks, cutlets or fillets. It is now widely farmed, which produces fish with a softer texture and less flavour. Wild salmon is available in season. Pacific and Alaskan salmon are usually canned. Smoked salmon is widely available as a whole side or in slices. It is usually eaten with no further cooking.

Salmon trout

A round fish, also known as sea trout, this is a freshwater fish that migrates to the sea to feed before returning to fresh water to spawn. It closely resembles brown trout in appearance. Smoked salmon trout is increasingly available as a whole side or in slices. It requires no further cooking.

Sardine

Sardines are actually young pilchards: thin, silvery fish weighing about 115g/4oz. They have a mass of fine scales that should be scraped off before cooking. They are widely available canned in oil.

Scallop

A fan-shaped shellfish, the scallop ranges in size from 7.5–18cm/ 3–7 inches across. There are many different varieties and they are available in their shells and shelled, fresh or frozen. The orange-coloured coral or roe is regarded as a delicacy.

Sea bass

A dark grey round fish that may weigh as much as 9kg/20lb, it is most often sold and cooked whole. The spiny dorsal fin and the scales must be removed before cooking.

Sea bream

This comprises a family of round fish, which vary in colour from dark grey through light grey to crimson. The last variety is also known as red porgy. It is quite different from and much better flavoured than freshwater bream. It is usually sold whole, weighing about 900g/2lb, but fillets are occasionally available.

Snapper

This comprises a family of round fish, varying in size from 15–90cm/ 6 inches–3 feet and in colour from red through orange to pink. It is available whole and in fillets.

Squid

Classed as seafood, squid is a member of the octopus family. It ranges in size from 5–25 cm/ 2–10 inches. It is sold whole and ready-prepared, fresh and frozen.

Trout

There are two varieties of this round freshwater fish – brown and rainbow. Brown trout are about 30cm/12 inches long and thought to have the better flavour, but may be difficult to obtain. Rainbow trout are iridescent with pink flesh. They are extensively farmed and usually sold whole or in fillets. Smoked trout is also widely available as whole fish and in fillets. It needs no further cooking.

Tuna

A round fish of the mackerel family, tuna ranges in size from about 675g/2½lb to over 450kg/1,000lb. Fresh tuna is usually sold as steaks. It is widely available canned in oil or brine.

Whitebait

These tiny round fish, the young of herring or sprats, are about 5cm/ 2 inches long. They are sold and cooked whole.

Buying and Storing

A shining skin, bright colour, pink gills and full bright eyes with black pupils and transparent corneas are the signs of fresh fish. The body should feel firm and springy. It should have a clean, pleasant smell, not a nasty "fishy" odour. The scales should be clearly in place.

Shellfish deteriorates very quickly, so if it is not fresh, your nose will inform you immediately.

Many types of shellfish, such as clams and mussels, are sold live to ensure freshness. Crab may also be sold live and is available ready-cooked. When preparing live mussels, clams or other shellfish, discard any that have damaged shells or that do not close at once when sharply tapped with the back of a knife. These are already dead and will contaminate the dish.

Discard any that have not opened by the end of cooking.

Ideally, fish should be cooked and eaten on the day of purchase. It may be stored in the refrigerator for a maximum of one day. Wrap it loosely in greaseproof paper or foil to prevent its smell penetrating other foods. If not alive, seafood should always be cooked and eaten on the day of purchase.

Poaching

Whole fish, large and small, as well as fillets, cutlets and steaks, are excellent poached because the gentle cooking gives succulent results. Poached fish can be served hot or cold with a wide variety of sauces. The poaching liquid may be used as a basis for the sauce.

1 To oven poach small, whole fish, fillets, cutlets or steaks, place the fish in a buttered, flame-proof dish that is large enough to hold the pieces in a single layer. Pour in enough liquid to come two-thirds of the way up the sides of the fish.

2 Add any flavourings specified in the recipe. Press a piece of buttered, greaseproof paper on top to keep in the moisture.

3 Set the dish over moderate heat and bring the liquid just to the boil. Transfer the dish to a preheated oven at 180°C/350°F/ Gas 4 and poach until the fish is just cooked. To test, with the tip of a sharp knife, make a small cut into the thickest part of the fish, ideally near a bone. The flesh should be slightly translucent.

4 To poach whole fish, fillets, cutlets or steaks on the hob, put large whole fish on the rack in a fish kettle or set on a piece of muslin that can be used like a hammock. Small whole fish, fillets, cutlets and steaks may be poached in a fish kettle on a rack or set directly in a wide saucepan or frying pan.

5 Prepare the poaching liquid – water, milk, wine or stock – in the fish kettle, a large casserole, a roasting tin, a wide saucepan or frying pan, as appropriate. Set the rack in the kettle or the muslin hammock in the casserole or tin. Add more liquid if necessary.

6 Cover the kettle or casserole and bring the liquid just to the boil. Reduce the heat and simmer very gently until the fish is cooked.

Steaming

This simple, moist-heat method of cooking is ideal for fish and shellfish. If you do not have a steamer, it is easy to improvise.

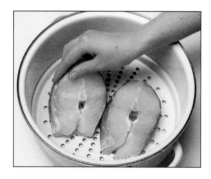

1 Using a steamer, arrange the fish on the rack in the steamer and set over boiling water. Cover and steam until done.

2 For Chinese-style steaming, arrange the fish on a heatproof plate that will fit inside a bamboo steamer or wok. Put the plate in the steamer or on the rack in the wok, set over boiling water, cover and steam until done.

3 For steaming larger fish and fillets, arrange the fish on a rack in a roasting tin of boiling water or on a plate set on the rack. Cover tightly with foil and steam until done.

4 To steam in foil, wrap the fish and seasonings in foil, sealing well, and set on a rack in the steamer or in a large roasting tin of boiling water. Steam until done.

Grilling

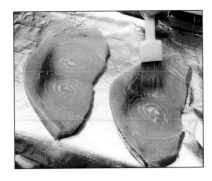

1 To grill small, whole oily fish, boned and butterflied fish, fillets, cutlets and steaks that are at least 1cm/½in thick or cubes of fish on skewers, rinse the fish and pat it dry with kitchen paper. Marinate the fish if the recipe suggests this.

2 Preheat the grill with the grill pan in place. When hot, lightly brush the hot pan with oil. Arrange the fish in the pan in a single layer, skin side down, brush the fish with butter, oil or a basting mixture, according to the recipe.

3 Set the fish under the grill, 7.5–10cm/3–4in from the heat. Thin pieces should be closer to the heat for a shorter time than thicker ones. Grill, basting once or twice and turning if the recipe specifies, until the fish is done.

4 To grill leaner, small whole fish, steaks, cutlets and fillets that are at least 1cm/½in thick and prepared for cooking as above, arrange in a buttered, flameproof dish. Add a little liquid – wine, stock or court bouillon – just to cover the base of the dish. Brush the fish with butter, oil or a basting mixture, according to the recipe. Grill as above, without turning the fish.

Coating and Frying

1 Lightly beat an egg in a shallow dish. Spread some flour on a plate or sheet of grease-proof paper and season with salt and freshly ground black pepper or ingredients as specified in the recipe. Spread fine breadcrumbs or crushed water biscuits on another plate or sheet of greaseproof paper.

2 To egg and crumb large pieces of fish, dip the fish first in the seasoned flour, turning to coat both sides lightly and evenly. Shake or brush off excess flour.

3 Next, dip the floured fish in the egg, turning to moisten both sides.

4 Dip the fish in the crumbs, turning to coat evenly. Press to help the crumbs adhere. Shake or pat off excess crumbs. Chill in the refrigerator for at least 20 minutes to set the coating.

5 To egg and crumb small pieces of fish, strips of fish fillet, goujons or prawns, put the crumbs in a plastic bag. After dipping the fish in seasoned flour and egg, toss a few pieces at a time in the plastic bag of crumbs.

6 To pan fry, heat some oil or a mixture of oil and butter in a frying pan, using enough to coat the base of the pan in a thin layer or according to recipe instructions. When it is very hot, put the fish in the pan in a single layer. Fry until golden brown on both sides and the fish is done. Drain on kitchen paper before serving.

7 To deep-fry, half fill a deep pan with oil and heat it to 190°C/375°F. Gently lower the coated pieces of fish into the hot oil, frying them only a few at a time. Fry until golden brown, turning them occasionally, so that they cook evenly. Remove and drain thoroughly on kitchen paper before serving.

SOUPS &
STARTERS

Corn and Crab Meat Soup

This soup originated in the United States, but it has since been introduced into China. You must use creamed corn in the recipe to achieve the right consistency.

INGREDIENTS

Serves 4

115g/4oz crab meat or chicken breast fillet

10ml/2 tsp finely chopped fresh
   root ginger

2 egg whites

30ml/2 tbsp milk

15ml/1 tbsp cornflour paste

600ml/1 pint/2½ cups vegetable or
   chicken stock

225g/8oz can creamed sweetcorn

salt and freshly ground black pepper

finely chopped spring onions, to garnish

1 Flake the crab meat (or roughly chop the chicken breast) and mix with the ginger.

2 Beat the egg whites until frothy, add the milk and cornflour paste and beat again until smooth. Blend with the crab meat or chicken breast.

3 In a wok or saucepan, bring the stock to the boil, add the creamed sweetcorn and bring back to the boil.

4 Stir in the crab meat or chicken breast and egg-white mixture, adjust the seasonings and stir gently until well blended and the meat is cooked. Serve garnished with finely chopped spring onions.

Crab and Egg Noodle Broth

This delicious broth is the perfect solution when you are hungry, time is short, and you need something fast, nutritious and filling.

INGREDIENTS

Serves 4

75g/3oz fine egg noodles

25g/1oz unsalted butter

1 small bunch spring onions, chopped

1 celery stick, sliced

1 medium carrot, peeled and cut into batons

1.2 litres/2 pints/5 cups chicken stock

60ml/4 tbsp dry sherry

115g/4oz white crab meat, fresh or frozen

pinch of celery salt

pinch of cayenne pepper

10ml/2 tsp lemon juice

1 small bunch coriander or flat leaf parsley, to garnish

3 Add the chicken stock and sherry to the pan, bring to the boil, reduce the heat and simmer for a further 5 minutes.

4 If using frozen crab meat, allow it to thaw. Flake the crab meat between your fingers on to a plate and remove any stray pieces of shell.

5 Drain the noodles and add to the broth, together with the crab meat. Season to taste with celery salt and cayenne pepper and sharpen with the lemon juice. Return to a simmer.

6 Ladle the broth into shallow soup plates, scatter with roughly chopped coriander or parsley and serve.

1 Bring a large saucepan of water to the boil. Toss in the egg noodles and cook according to the instructions on the packet. Cool under cold running water and leave immersed in water until required.

2 Heat the butter in another large pan, add the spring onions, celery and carrot, cover and soften the vegetables over a gentle heat for 3–4 minutes.

Clam Chowder

Clams canned or bottled in brine can be used instead of fresh ones.

INGREDIENTS

Serves 4

300ml/½ pint/1¼ cups double cream

75g/3oz unsalted butter

1 small onion, finely chopped

1 apple, sliced

1 garlic clove, crushed

45ml/3 tbsp mild curry powder

350g/12oz baby sweetcorn

600ml/1 pint/2½ cups fish stock

225g/8oz new potatoes, peeled and cooked

24 baby onions, peeled and boiled

40 small fresh clams

salt and freshly ground black pepper

8 lime wedges, to garnish

1 Pour the cream into a small saucepan and cook over a high heat until it is reduced by half.

2 Melt half the butter in another pan. Sauté the onion, apple, garlic and curry powder over a low heat until the onion is translucent but not coloured . Stir in the reduced cream.

3 Melt the remaining butter in another saucepan. Add the baby sweetcorn and cook for 5 minutes. Increase the heat and add the cream mixture and stock. Bring to the boil.

4 Add the potatoes, baby onions and clams. Cover and cook until the clams have opened. Discard any that do not open. Season well to taste and serve, garnished with the lime wedges.

Seafood Soup with Rouille

This is a really chunky aromatic mixed fish soup from Provence, flavoured with plenty of saffron and herbs. Rouille, a fiery hot paste, is served separately for everyone to swirl into their soup to flavour. It means rust, which describes the brilliant red colour resulting from the chilli and pepper. Saffron is also sometimes included.

INGREDIENTS

Serves 6

3 gurnard or red mullet, filleted

12 large raw or cooked prawns

675g/1½lb white fish fillets, such as cod, haddock, halibut or monkfish

225g/8oz fresh mussels

5ml/1 tsp saffron strands

15ml/1 tbsp boiling water

75ml/5 tbsp olive oil

1 fennel bulb, roughly chopped

4 garlic cloves, crushed

3 strips orange rind

4 thyme sprigs

1.2 litres/2 pints/5 cups fish stock

400g/14oz can chopped tomatoes

30ml/2 tbsp sun-dried tomato paste

3 bay leaves

salt and freshly ground black pepper

For the rouille

1 red pepper, seeded and roughly chopped

1 red chilli, seeded and sliced

2 garlic cloves, chopped

75ml/5 tbsp olive oil

15g/½oz fresh breadcrumbs

1 First make the rouille. Put the pepper, chilli, garlic, oil and breadcrumbs in a blender or food processor and process until smooth. Transfer the rouille to a serving dish and chill in the refrigerator until required.

2 Cut the gurnard or red mullet fillets into large chunks. Peel half the prawns. Skin the white fish fillets, remove any remaining bones and cut the flesh into large chunks. Debeard and scrub the mussels well under cold running water, discarding any damaged ones and any that do not close immediately when tapped sharply with the back of a knife.

3 Soak the saffron strands in the boiling water. Meanwhile, heat 30ml/2 tbsp of the olive oil in a large sauté pan or saucepan. Add the gurnard or mullet and white fish chunks and fry over a high heat for 1 minute. Remove from the pan and drain.

4 Add the remaining oil to the pan and return to the heat. Add the fennel, garlic, orange rind and thyme and fry, stirring from time to time, until the fennel and garlic begin to colour.

5 Add the stock to the pan, together with the saffron liquid, tomatoes, sun-dried tomato paste and bay leaves. Season to taste with salt and pepper. Bring almost to the boil, lower the heat, cover and simmer for 15 minutes.

6 Stir in the gurnard or mullet chunks, white fish chunks, peeled and unpeeled prawns and the mussels. Cover and cook for 3–4 minutes. Discard any mussels that do not open. Serve the soup hot with the rouille.

COOK'S TIP

If you prefer a milder-tasting accompaniment, substitute the equally authentic Provençal paste called pistou. This is very similar to Italian pesto. Skin and seed 2 very ripe, large tomatoes and roughly chop the flesh. Pound together the tomato flesh, 5 garlic cloves, 25g/1oz fresh basil leaves and 75g/3oz freshly grated Parmesan cheese in a mortar with a pestle. Transfer to a bowl and gradually beat in 60 ml/ 4 tbsp olive oil until fully incorporated. Alternatively, process the tomatoes, garlic, basil and cheese in a food processor until smooth. With the motor still running, gradually add the olive oil. Stir the pistou into the soup before serving or hand round separately.

Deep-fried Whitebait

A spicy coating on these fish gives this favourite dish a crunchy bite.

Serves 6

115g/4oz plain flour

2.5ml/½ tsp curry powder

2.5ml/½ tsp ground ginger

2.5ml/½ tsp ground cayenne pepper

pinch of salt

1.1kg/2½lb fresh or frozen
   whitebait, thawed

vegetable oil for deep-frying

lemon wedges, to garnish

1 Mix together the flour, spices and salt in a large bowl.

2 Coat the fish in the seasoned flour and shake off any excess.

3 Heat the oil in a large, heavy-based saucepan until it reaches a temperature of 190°C/375°F. Fry the whitebait in batches for about 2–3 minutes until the fish is golden and crispy.

4 Drain well on absorbent kitchen paper. Serve hot, garnished with lemon wedges.

Smoked Salmon Pancakes with Pesto

These simple pancakes take no more than 10–15 minutes to prepare and are perfect for a special occasion. Smoked salmon is delicious with fresh basil and combines well with toasted pine nuts and a spoonful of crème fraîche.

INGREDIENTS

Makes 12–16

120ml/4fl oz/½ cup milk

115g/4oz self-raising flour

1 egg

30ml/2 tbsp pesto sauce

vegetable oil, for frying

200ml/7fl oz/scant 1 cup crème fraîche

75g/3oz smoked salmon

15g/½oz pine nuts, toasted

salt and freshly ground black pepper

12–16 fresh basil sprigs, to garnish

3 Heat the vegetable oil in a large frying pan. Spoon the pancake mixture into the heated oil in small heaps. Allow about 30 seconds for the pancakes to rise, then turn and cook briefly on the other side. Keep warm. Continue cooking the pancakes in batches until all the batter has been used up.

4 Arrange the pancakes on a serving plate and top each one with a spoonful of crème fraîche.

5 Cut the salmon into 1cm/½ in strips and place on top of each pancake. Scatter each pancake with pine nuts and garnish with a sprig of fresh basil.

1 Pour half of the milk into a mixing bowl. Add the flour, egg, pesto sauce and seasoning and mix to a smooth batter.

2 Add the remainder of the milk and stir until evenly blended.

Sautéed Scallops

Scallops go well with all sorts of sauces, but simple cooking is the best way to enjoy their flavour.

INGREDIENTS

Serves 2

450g/1lb shelled scallops

25g/1oz butter

30ml/2 tbsp dry white vermouth

15ml/1 tbsp finely chopped fresh parsley

salt and freshly ground black pepper

1 Rinse the scallops under cold running water to remove any sand or grit and pat dry using kitchen paper. Season them lightly with salt and pepper.

2 In a frying pan large enough to hold the scallops in one layer, heat half the butter until it begins to colour. Sauté the scallops for 3–5 minutes, turning, until golden brown on both sides and just firm to the touch. Remove to a serving platter and cover to keep warm.

3 Add the vermouth to the hot frying pan, swirl in the remaining butter, add the parsley and pour the sauce over the scallops. Serve immediately.

Garlicky Scallops and Prawns

Scallops and prawns are found all along the Atlantic and Mediterranean coasts of France and are enjoyed in every region. This method of cooking is a typical Provençal recipe.

INGREDIENTS

Serves 2–4

6 large shelled scallops

6–8 large raw prawns, peeled

plain flour, for dusting

30–45ml/2–3 tbsp olive oil

1 garlic clove, finely chopped

15ml/1 tbsp chopped fresh basil

30–45ml/2–3 tbsp lemon juice

salt and freshly ground black pepper

1 Rinse the scallops under cold running water to remove any sand or grit. Pat them dry using kitchen paper and cut in half crossways. Season the scallops and prawns with salt and pepper and dust lightly with flour, shaking off the excess.

2 Heat the oil in a large frying pan over a high heat and add the scallops and prawns.

3 Reduce the heat to medium-high and cook for 2 minutes, then turn the scallops and prawns. Add the garlic and basil, shaking the pan to distribute them evenly. Cook for a further 2 minutes until the scallops are golden and just firm to the touch. Sprinkle over the lemon juice and toss to blend.

VARIATION

To make a richer sauce, transfer the cooked scallops and prawns to a warmed plate. Pour 60ml/ 4 tbsp dry white wine into the frying pan and boil to reduce by half. Add 15g/½oz unsalted butter, whisking until it melts and the sauce thickens slightly. Pour over the scallops and prawns and serve.

Grilled Green Mussels with Cumin

Green-shelled mussels have a more distinctive flavour than the small, black variety. Keep the empty shells to use as individual salt and pepper holders for fishy meals.

INGREDIENTS

Serves 4

45ml/3 tbsp fresh parsley

45ml/3 tbsp fresh coriander

1 garlic clove, crushed

pinch of ground cumin

25g/1oz unsalted butter, softened

25g/1oz brown breadcrumbs

12 green mussels or 24 small mussels, on the half-shell

freshly ground black pepper

chopped fresh parsley, to garnish

1 Finely chop the fresh parsley and coriander.

2 Beat the garlic, herbs, cumin and butter together with a wooden spoon.

3 Stir in the breadcrumbs and freshly ground black pepper.

4 Spoon a little of the mixture on to each mussel and grill for 2 minutes. Serve garnished with chopped, fresh parsley.

Glazed Garlic Prawns

This is a fairly simple and quick dish to prepare. It is best to peel the prawns, as this helps them to absorb maximum flavour. Serve with a salad as an appetizer or as a main course with a selection of vegetables and other accompaniments .

INGREDIENTS

Serves 4

15ml/1 tbsp vegetable oil

3 garlic cloves, roughly chopped

3 tomatoes, chopped

2.5ml/½ tsp salt

5ml/1 tsp crushed dried red chillies

5ml/1 tsp lemon juice

15ml/1 tbsp mango chutney

1 fresh green chilli, chopped

15–20 cooked king prawns, peeled
   and deveined

fresh coriander sprigs, 4 unpeeled, cooked
   king prawns (optional) and 2 spring
   onions, chopped (optional), to garnish

1 In a medium saucepan, heat the oil and add the chopped garlic cloves.

2 Lower the heat and add the chopped tomatoes along with the salt, crushed chillies, lemon juice, mango chutney and chopped fresh chilli.

3 Finally, add the prawns, turn up the heat and stir-fry them quickly, until heated through.

4 Transfer to a warmed serving dish. Serve garnished with fresh coriander, unpeeled king prawns and chopped spring onions, if liked.

COOK'S TIP

This is a very fiery dish – if you would prefer it less hot, carefully seed the chilli before chopping and reduce the crushed chillies to a pinch .

Sole Goujons with Lime Mayonnaise

This simple dish can be rustled up very quickly. It also makes an excellent light lunch or supper.

INGREDIENTS

Serves 4

200ml/7fl oz/scant 1 cup mayonnaise

1 small garlic clove, crushed

10ml/2 tsp capers, rinsed and chopped

10ml/2 tsp chopped gherkins

grated rind and juice of 1 lime

15ml/1 tbsp finely chopped
    fresh coriander

675g/1½lb sole fillets, skinned

2 eggs, beaten

115g/4oz/2 cups fresh white breadcrumbs

oil, for deep-frying

salt and freshly ground black pepper

lime wedges, to serve

1 To make the lime mayonnaise, mix together the mayonnaise, garlic, capers, gherkins, lime rind and juice and chopped coriander. Season with salt and pepper to taste. Transfer to a serving bowl and chill until required.

2 Cut the sole fillets into finger-length strips. Dip each strip first into the beaten egg, then into the breadcrumbs.

3 Heat the oil in a deep-fat fryer to 180°C/350°F. Add the fish strips, in batches, and fry until they are golden brown and crisp. Drain well on kitchen paper and keep warm while you cook the remaining strips.

4 Pile the goujons on to warmed serving plates and serve with the lime wedges for squeezing over. Hand the sauce round separately.

Spicy Fish Rösti

You can also serve these fish cakes crisp and hot for lunch or supper with a mixed green salad.

INGREDIENTS

Serves 4

350g/12oz large, firm waxy potatoes

350g/12oz salmon or cod fillet, skinned
    and boned

3–4 spring onions, finely chopped

5ml/1 tsp grated fresh root ginger

30ml/2 tbsp chopped fresh coriander

10ml/2 tsp lemon juice

30–45ml/2–3 tbsp sunflower oil

salt and cayenne pepper

coriander sprigs, to garnish

lemon wedges, to serve

1 Cook the potatoes with their skins on in a pan of boiling salted water for 10 minutes. Drain and leave to cool for a few minutes.

2 Meanwhile, finely chop the salmon or cod fillet and put into a bowl. Stir in the chopped spring onions, grated root ginger, chopped coriander and lemon juice. Season to taste with salt and cayenne pepper.

3 When the potatoes are cool enough to handle, peel off the skins and grate the potatoes coarsely. Gently stir the grated potato into the fish mixture.

4 Form the fish mixture into 12 cakes, pressing the mixture together and leaving the edges slightly rough.

5 Heat the oil in a large frying pan and fry the fish cakes, a few at a time, for 3 minutes on each side, until golden brown and crisp. Drain on kitchen paper. Serve hot, garnished with sprigs of coriander and with lemon wedges for squeezing over.

Welsh Rarebit with Anchovies

A classic snack or starter adapted to include salty anchovies. Make as required because the sauce will not keep for long.

INGREDIENTS

Serves 4

40g/1½oz canned anchovies, drained

175g/6oz butter

6 slices of bread, crusts removed

4 large egg yolks

300ml/½ pint/1¼ cups double cream

pinch of cayenne pepper

salt and freshly ground black pepper

15ml/1 tbsp chopped fresh parsley,
    to garnish

1 In a food processor fitted with a metal blade, process the anchovy fillets with two-thirds of the butter. Toast the bread, spread with the anchovy butter, set aside and keep warm.

COOK'S TIP

If you find canned anchovies too salty, soak them briefly in cold water before processing them with the butter.

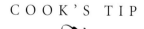

2 Melt the remaining butter in a small, heavy-based saucepan and beat in the egg yolks.

3 Take off the heat and add the cream. Season to taste, then replace on a low heat. Stir continuously until the sauce is thick. Pour over the toast and sprinkle with the cayenne pepper. Garnish with the chopped fresh parsley.

Seafood Wontons with Coriander Dressing

These tasty wontons resemble tortellini. Water chestnuts add a light crunch to the filling.

INGREDIENTS

Serves 4

225g/8oz cooked prawns, peeled
    and deveined
115g/4oz white crab meat
4 canned water chestnuts, finely diced
1 spring onion, finely chopped
1 small green chilli, seeded and
    finely chopped
1.5ml/¼ tsp grated fresh root ginger
1 egg, separated
20–24 wonton wrappers
salt and freshly ground black pepper
coriander leaves, to garnish

For the coriander dressing

30ml/2 tbsp rice vinegar
15ml/1 tbsp chopped, pickled ginger
90ml/6 tbsp olive oil
15ml/1 tbsp soy sauce
45ml/3 tbsp chopped coriander
30ml/2 tbsp finely diced red pepper

1 Finely dice the prawns and place them in a bowl. Add the crab meat, water chestnuts, spring onion, chilli, ginger and egg white. Season with salt and pepper to taste and stir well.

2 Place a wonton wrapper on a board. Put about 5ml/1 tsp of the filling just above the centre of the wrapper. With a pastry brush, moisten the edges of the wrapper with a little of the egg yolk. Bring the bottom of the wrapper up over the filling. Press gently to expel any air, then seal the wrapper neatly in a triangle.

3 For a more elaborate shape, bring the two side points up over the filling, overlap the points and pinch the ends firmly together. Space the filled wontons on a large baking sheet lined with grease-proof paper, so that they do not stick together.

4 Half fill a large saucepan with water. Bring to simmering point. Add the filled wontons, a few at a time, and simmer for about 2–3 minutes, or until the wontons float to the surface. When ready, the wrappers will be translu-cent and the filling should be cooked. Remove the wontons with a large slotted spoon, drain them briefly, then spread them on trays. Keep warm while you cook the remaining wontons.

5 Make the coriander dressing by whisking all the ingredients together in a bowl. Divide the wontons among serving dishes, drizzle with the dressing and serve, garnished with a handful of coriander leaves.

FISH
DISHES

Hoki Balls in Tomato Sauce

This quick meal is a good choice for young children, as you can guarantee no bones. Its low fat content also makes it an ideal dish for anyone on a low-fat or low-cholesterol diet. If you like, add a dash of chilli sauce.

INGREDIENTS

Serves 4

450g/1lb hoki or other white fish
    fillets, skinned
60ml/4 tbsp fresh wholemeal
    breadcrumbs
30ml/2 tbsp snipped chives or
    spring onion
400g/14oz can chopped tomatoes
50g/2oz button mushrooms, sliced
salt and freshly ground black pepper
fresh chives, to garnish

1 Cut the fish fillets into large chunks and place in a food processor. Add the wholemeal breadcrumbs, chives or spring onion. Season to taste with salt and pepper and process until the fish is finely chopped, but still has some texture left.

COOK'S TIP

Hoki is a good choice for this dish, but if it is not available, use cod, haddock or whiting instead.

2 Divide the fish mixture into about 16 even-sized pieces, then mould them into balls with your hands.

3 Place the tomatoes and mushrooms in a large saucepan and cook over a medium heat until boiling. Carefully add the fish balls, cover and simmer for about 10 minutes, until cooked. Serve hot, garnished with chives.

Cod with Caper Sauce

This quick and easy sauce, with a slightly sharp and 'nutty' flavour, is a very effective way of enhancing rather bland fish.

INGREDIENTS

Serves 4

4 cod steaks, about 175g/6oz each
115g/4oz butter
15ml/1 tbsp vinegar
15ml/1 tbsp capers
15ml/1 tbsp chopped fresh parsley
salt and freshly ground black pepper
tarragon sprigs, to garnish

1 Season the cod with salt and pepper to taste. Melt 25g/1oz of the butter, then brush some over one side of each piece of cod.

2 Cook the cod under a preheated grill for about 6 minutes, turn it over, brush with more melted butter and cook for a further 5–6 minutes, or until the fish flakes easily.

3 Meanwhile, heat the remaining butter until it turns golden brown, but do not allow it to burn. Add the vinegar, followed by the capers, and stir well.

4 Pour the vinegar, butter and capers over the fish, sprinkle with parsley and garnish with the tarragon sprigs.

COOK'S TIP

Thick tail fillets of cod or haddock could be used in place of the cod steaks, if you prefer.

Breaded Fish with Tartare Sauce

All the taste of the classic British fish dish but without any frying.

INGREDIENTS

Serves 4

50g/2oz dried breadcrumbs

5ml/1 tsp dried oregano

2.5ml/½ tsp cayenne pepper

250ml/8fl oz/1 cup milk

10ml/2 tsp salt

4 pieces of cod fillet, about 675g/1½lb

40g/1½oz butter or margarine, melted

For the tartare sauce

120ml/4fl oz/½ cup mayonnaise

2.5ml/½ tsp Dijon mustard

1–2 pickled gherkins, finely chopped

15ml/1 tbsp drained capers, chopped

5ml/1 tsp chopped fresh parsley

5ml/1 tsp chopped fresh chives

5ml/1 tsp chopped fresh tarragon

salt and freshly ground black pepper

2 Dip the pieces of cod fillet in the milk, then transfer to the plate and coat with the breadcrumb mixture.

3 Arrange the coated fish in the prepared baking dish, in a single layer. Drizzle the melted butter or margarine over the fish.

4 Bake in a preheated oven at 230°C/450°F/Gas 8 for about 10–15 minutes, until the fish flakes easily when tested with a fork.

5 Meanwhile, combine all the ingredients for the tartare sauce in a small bowl. Stir gently to mix thoroughly. Serve the fish hot, accompanied by the tartare sauce, handed separately.

1 Grease a shallow ovenproof baking dish. Combine the breadcrumbs, oregano and cayenne pepper on a plate and blend together. Mix the milk with the salt in a bowl, stirring well to dissolve the salt.

Chunky Fish Balti with Peppers

Try to find as many differently coloured sweet peppers as possible to make this very attractive dish.

INGREDIENTS

Serves 2–4

450g/1lb cod, or any other firm, white fish

7.5ml/1½ tsp ground cumin

10ml/2 tsp mango powder

5ml/1 tsp ground coriander

2.5ml/½ tsp chilli powder

5ml/1 tsp salt

5ml/1 tsp ginger pulp

45ml/3 tbsp cornflour

150ml/¼ pint/⅔ cup corn oil

3 coloured peppers, seeded and chopped

8–10 cherry tomatoes

1 Skin the fish and cut it into small cubes. Put the fish cubes into a large mixing bowl and add the ground cumin, mango powder, ground coriander, chilli powder, salt, ginger pulp and cornflour. Mix together thoroughly, using 2 spoons or your hands, until the fish is well coated.

2 Heat the oil in a preheated wok or karahi. Lower the heat and add the fish pieces, 3 or 4 at a time. Fry for about 3 minutes, turning and moving them constantly.

3 Drain the fish on kitchen paper. Transfer to a serving dish and keep warm while you fry the remaining fish pieces.

4 Add the peppers to the wok or karahi and fry for 2 minutes. They should still be slightly crisp. Drain on kitchen paper.

5 Add the peppers to the serving dish and garnish with the cherry tomatoes. Serve at once.

Fried Fish with Piquant Mayonnaise

This sauce makes fried fish just that extra bit special.

INGREDIENTS

Serves 4

1 egg

45ml/3 tbsp olive oil

squeeze of lemon juice

2.5ml/½ tsp finely chopped fresh dill
   or parsley

4 whiting or haddock fillets

50g/2oz plain flour

25g/1oz butter or margarine

salt and freshly ground black pepper

mixed salad, to serve

For the mayonnaise

1 egg yolk

30ml/2 tbsp Dijon mustard

30ml/2 tbsp white wine vinegar

10ml/2 tsp paprika

300ml/½ pint/1¼ cups olive or
   vegetable oil

30ml/2 tbsp creamed horseradish

1 garlic clove, finely chopped

25g/1oz finely chopped celery

30ml/2 tbsp tomato ketchup

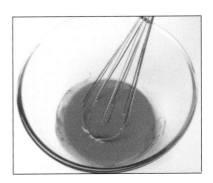

1 To make the mayonnaise, blend the egg yolk, mustard, vinegar and paprika in a mixing bowl. Add the oil in a thin stream, beating vigorously with a wire whisk to blend it in.

2 When the mixture is smooth and thick, beat in all the other mayonnaise ingredients. Cover and chill until ready to serve.

3 Combine the egg, 15ml/1 tbsp of the olive oil, the lemon juice, the dill or parsley and a little salt and pepper in a shallow dish. Beat until well mixed.

4 Dip both sides of each fish fillet in the egg and herb mixture, then coat the fillets lightly and evenly with flour, shaking off the excess.

5 Heat the butter or margarine with the remaining olive oil in a large, heavy-based frying pan. Fry the coated fish fillets for 8–10 minutes, until golden brown on both sides and cooked through. If necessary, cook the fish in two batches, keeping the cooked fish warm while you are cooking the remainder.

6 Serve the fish hot, with the piquant mayonnaise and accompanied by a salad.

Haddock and Broccoli Stew

This is an easy, one-pot meal full of colour and texture.

INGREDIENTS

Serves 4

4 spring onions, sliced

450g/1lb new potatoes, diced

300ml/½ pint/1¼ cups fish stock or water

300ml/½ pint/1¼ cups milk

1 bay leaf

225g/8oz broccoli florets, sliced

450g/1lb smoked haddock fillets, skinned

200g/7oz can sweetcorn, drained

freshly ground black pepper

chopped spring onions, to garnish

crusty bread, to serve

1 Place the spring onions and potatoes in a large saucepan and add the stock or water, milk and bay leaf. Bring the mixture to the boil, then cover the pan and simmer for 10 minutes.

2 Add the broccoli to the pan. Cut the fish into bite-sized chunks and add to the pan with the sweetcorn.

3 Season the stew well with black pepper, then cover the pan and simmer for a further 5 minutes, or until the fish is cooked through. Remove the bay leaf and transfer to a serving dish. Scatter over the spring onion and serve hot with crusty bread.

COOK'S TIP

When new potatoes are not available, old ones can be used, but choose a waxy variety which will not disintegrate.

Haddock with Leek Sauté

Instead of the classic cheese sauce, this Gruyère-topped leek sauté allows the fresh taste of the haddock fillet to dominate. Garnish with long chives for this clever lattice effect.

INGREDIENTS

Serves 4

4 x 225g/8oz haddock fillets
675g/1½lb leeks
1 onion
50g/2oz butter
5ml/1 tsp caraway seeds
50g/2oz finely grated Gruyère cheese
salt and freshly ground black pepper
long chives, to garnish (optional)

1 Season the fish with salt and pepper. Preheat the grill.

2 With a sharp knife, cut the leeks into 1cm/½ inch thick diagonal slices. Roughly chop the onion.

3 Melt the butter in a large, heavy-based saucepan and sauté the leeks and onion until soft. Stir in the caraway seeds.

4 Line the base of a flameproof dish with the vegetable mixture. Sprinkle over the grated cheese and top with the haddock fillets. Grill for 10–15 minutes, until cooked. Serve hot, garnished with a lattice of long chives, if wished.

Turbot in Parchment

Cooking in parcels is not new, but it is an ideal way to cook fish. Serve this dish plain or with a little hollandaise sauce and let each person open their own parcel to savour the aroma.

INGREDIENTS

Serves 4

2 carrots, cut into thin julienne strips

2 courgettes, cut into thin julienne strips

2 leeks, cut into thin julienne strips

1 fennel bulb, cut into thin julienne strips

2 tomatoes, skinned, seeded and diced

30ml/2 tbsp chopped fresh dill, tarragon, or chervil

4 turbot fillets, about 200g/7oz each, cut in half

20ml/4 tsp olive oil

60ml/4 tbsp white wine or fish stock

salt and freshly ground black pepper

1 Cut 4 pieces of non-stick baking paper, about 45cm/18in long. Fold each piece in half and cut into a heart shape.

2 Open the paper hearts. Arrange one quarter of each of the vegetables next to the fold of each heart. Sprinkle with salt and pepper and half the chopped herbs. Arrange 2 pieces of turbot fillet over each bed of vegetables, overlapping the thin end of one piece and the thicker end of the other. Sprinkle the remaining herbs, the olive oil and wine or stock evenly over the fish.

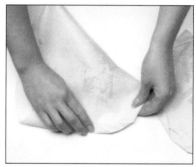

3 Fold the top half of one of the paper hearts over the fish and vegetables and, beginning at the rounded end, fold the edges of the paper over, twisting and folding to form an airtight packet. Repeat with the remaining three.

4 Slide the parcels on to one or two baking sheets and bake in a preheated oven at 190°C/375°F/Gas 5 for about 10 minutes, or until the paper is lightly browned and well puffed up. Slide each parcel on to a warmed serving plate and serve at once.

Fillets of Hake Baked with Thyme

Quick cooking is the essence of this dish. Use the freshest garlic available and, if there is no fresh thyme, use half the amount of dried thyme.

INGREDIENTS

Serves 4

4 x 175g/6oz hake fillets

1 shallot, finely chopped

2 garlic cloves, thinly sliced

4 fresh thyme sprigs

grated rind and juice of 1 lemon, plus
    extra juice for drizzling

30ml/2 tbsp extra virgin olive oil

salt and freshly ground black pepper

finely grated lemon rind and fresh thyme
    sprigs, to garnish

1 Arrange the hake fillets on the base of a large roasting tin. Scatter the shallot, garlic cloves and thyme on top.

COOK'S TIP

Hake is a round fish extensively found in the North and South Atlantic and is extremely popular in Spain and Portugal. Its milky white flesh is delicate in flavour and quite fragile, so fillets need very careful handling, as they break up easily.

2 Season well with salt and freshly ground pepper.

3 Drizzle over the lemon juice and olive oil. Bake in a preheated oven at 180°C/350°F/ Gas 4 for about 15 minutes, or until the fish flakes easily. Serve, garnished with finely grated lemon rind and fresh thyme sprigs.

VARIATIONS

If hake is not available, you can use cod or haddock fillets for this recipe. You can also use a mixture of fresh herbs, such as tarragon, parsley and chervil.

Fish Steaks with Mustard Sauce

The simplest of dishes, this mustard sauce turns a plain fish into something special.

INGREDIENTS

Serves 4-6

4–6 halibut or turbot steaks, 2.5cm/ 1in thick

50g/2oz butter, melted

salt and freshly ground black pepper

frisée and lemon wedges, to garnish

For the mustard sauce

60ml/4 tbsp Dijon mustard

300ml/½ pint/1¼ cups double or whipping cream

2.5ml/½ tsp caster sugar

15ml/1 tbsp white wine vinegar or lemon juice

1 Season the fish steaks with salt and pepper. Arrange them on an oiled rack in the grill pan and brush the tops of the steaks with melted butter.

2 Cook under a preheated grill, about 10cm/4in from the heat, for about 4–5 minutes on each side, or until cooked through. Brush with more melted butter, when you turn the steaks.

3 Meanwhile, make the sauce. Combine the ingredients in a saucepan and bring to the boil, whisking constantly. Simmer, whisking, until the sauce thickens. Remove from the heat, set aside and keep warm.

4 Transfer the fish to warmed plates. Spoon over the sauce and serve immediately, garnished with frisée and lemon wedges.

Sea Bream with Orange Sauce

Sea bream is a taste revelation to anyone not yet familiar with its creamy rich flavour. The fish has a firm white flesh that scrumptiously partners a rich butter sauce, sharpened here with a dash of frozen orange juice concentrate.

INGREDIENTS

Serves 2

2 x 350g/12oz sea bream, scaled
   and gutted
10ml/2 tsp Dijon mustard
5ml/1 tsp fennel seeds
30ml/2 tbsp olive oil
50g/2oz watercress
175g/6oz mixed salad leaves, such as curly
   endive or frisée
jacket potatoes and orange slices, to serve

For the sauce

30ml/2 tbsp frozen orange
   juice concentrate
175g/6oz unsalted butter, diced
salt and cayenne pepper

1 Slash the bream diagonally four times on either side with a sharp knife. Combine the mustard and fennel seeds, then spread over both sides of the fish. Moisten with oil and cook under a preheated grill for 12 minutes, turning once.

2 Place the orange juice concentrate in a bowl and heat over 2.5cm/1in of boiling water. Remove the pan from the heat and gradually whisk the butter into the juice until creamy. Season, cover and set aside.

3 Moisten the watercress and salad leaves with the remaining olive oil. Arrange the fish on two large plates, spoon over the sauce and serve with the salad leaves, potatoes and orange slices.

COOK'S TIP

For speedy jacket potatoes, microwave small potatoes on 100% high power for 8 minutes, then crisp in a hot oven preheated to 200°C/400°F/Gas 6 for a further 10 minutes. Split, insert butter and serve.

Mackerel with Mustard and Lemon Butter

Look for bright, firm-looking really fresh mackerel.

INGREDIENTS

Serves 4

4 fresh mackerel, about 275g/10oz each, gutted and cleaned
175–225g/6–8oz young spinach leaves

For the mustard and lemon butter
115g/4oz butter, melted
30ml/2 tbsp wholegrain mustard
grated rind of 1 lemon
30ml/2 tbsp lemon juice
45ml/3 tbsp chopped fresh parsley
salt and freshly ground black pepper

1 To prepare each mackerel, cut off the heads just behind the gills, using a sharp knife, then cut along the belly so that the fish can be opened out flat.

2 Place the fish on a board, skin side up, and, with the heel of your hand, press along the backbone to loosen it.

3 Turn the fish the right way up and pull the bone away from the flesh. Remove the tail and cut each fish in half lengthways. Wash and pat dry.

4 Score the skin three or four times, then season the fish. To make the mustard and lemon butter, mix together the melted butter, mustard, lemon rind and juice, parsley and seasoning. Place the mackerel on a grill rack. Brush a little of the butter over the mackerel and grill for 5 minutes each side, basting occasionally, until cooked through.

5 Arrange the spinach leaves in the centre of 4 large plates. Place the mackerel on top. Heat the remaining butter in a small pan until sizzling and pour over the mackerel. Serve at once.

Tuna and Corn Fish Cakes

These economical little tuna fish cakes are quick to make. Use fresh mashed potatoes, or make a store cupboard version with instant mash.

INGREDIENTS

Serves 4

300g/11oz cooked mashed potatoes

200g/7oz can tuna fish in soya oil, drained and flaked

115g/4oz canned or frozen sweetcorn

30ml/2 tbsp chopped fresh parsley

50g/2oz fresh white or brown breadcrumbs

salt and freshly ground black pepper

lemon wedges, to garnish

fresh vegetables, to serve

1 Place the mashed potato in a bowl and stir in the tuna fish, sweetcorn and chopped parsley.

2 Season to taste with salt and pepper, then shape into 8 patty shapes with your hands.

3 Spread out the breadcrumbs on a plate and gently press the fish cakes into the breadcrumbs to coat lightly, then transfer to a baking sheet.

4 Cook the fish cakes under a moderately hot grill until crisp and golden brown, turning once. Serve hot with the lemon wedges and fresh vegetables.

COOK'S TIP

For simple store cupboard variations, which are just as nutritious, try using canned sardines, red or pink salmon, or smoked mackerel in place of the tuna fish.

Trout with Almonds

This simple and quick recipe doubles easily – you can cook the trout in two frying pans or in batches. In Normandy, hazelnuts might be used in place of almonds.

INGREDIENTS

Serves 2

2 trout, about 350g/12oz each, cleaned

40g/1½oz plain flour

50g/2oz butter

25g/1oz flaked or sliced almonds

30ml/2 tbsp dry white wine

salt and freshly ground black pepper

1 Rinse the trout and pat dry. Put the flour in a large polythene bag and season with salt and pepper. Place the trout, 1 at a time, in the bag and shake to coat with flour. Shake off the excess and discard the remaining flour.

2 Melt half the butter in a large frying pan over a medium heat. When it is foamy, add the trout and cook for 6–7 minutes on each side, until golden brown and the flesh next to the bone is opaque. Transfer the fish to warmed plates and keep warm.

3 Add the remaining butter to the pan and cook the almonds until just lightly browned. Add the wine to the pan and bring to the boil. Boil for 1 minute, stirring constantly, until slightly syrupy. Pour or spoon over the fish and serve at once.

St Rémy Tuna

St Rémy is a beautiful village in Provence in the South of France. Herbs, such as thyme, rosemary and oregano, grow wild on the nearby hillside and feature in many of the recipes from this area.

INGREDIENTS

Serves 4

4 tuna steaks, about 175–200g/6–7oz each, 2.5cm/1in thick

30–45ml/2–3 tbsp olive oil

3–4 garlic cloves, finely chopped

60ml/4 tbsp dry white wine

3 ripe plum tomatoes, skinned, seeded and chopped

5ml/1 tsp dried herbes de Provence

salt and freshly ground black pepper

fresh basil leaves, to garnish

fried potatoes, to serve

1 Season the tuna steaks with salt and pepper. Set a heavy frying pan over a high heat until very hot, add the oil and swirl to coat. Add the tuna steaks and press down gently, then reduce the heat to medium and cook for 6–8 minutes, turning once, until just slightly pink in the centre.

2 Transfer the steaks to a serving plate and cover to keep warm.

3 Add the garlic to the pan and fry for 15–20 seconds, stirring constantly, then pour in the wine and boil until it is reduced by half. Add the tomatoes and dried herbs and cook for 2–3 minutes until bubbling. Season with pepper and pour over the fish steaks. Garnish with fresh basil leaves and serve with fried potatoes.

COOK'S TIP

Tuna is often served pink in the middle, rather like beef. If you prefer it cooked through, reduce the heat and cook for an extra few minutes.

Fillets of Pink Trout with Tarragon Sauce

Trout fillets are increasingly available from supermarkets. Otherwise, buy four whole trout and ask your fishmonger to fillet and skin them for you.

INGREDIENTS

Serves 4

25g/1oz butter

8 trout fillets

salt and freshly ground black pepper

new potatoes and runner beans, to serve

For the tarragon sauce

2 large spring onions, white parts only, chopped

½ cucumber, peeled, seeded and cut into short batons

5ml/1 tsp cornflour

150ml/½ pint/⅔ cup single cream

50ml/2 fl oz/¼ cup dry sherry

30ml/2 tbsp chopped fresh tarragon

1 tomato, seeded and chopped

1 Melt the butter in a large frying pan. Season the trout fillets with salt and pepper and cook for about 6 minutes, turning once. Transfer the fillets to a plate, cover and keep warm.

2 To make the sauce, add the spring onions and cucumber batons to the same frying pan. Sauté over a low heat, stirring constantly, until they are soft, but not coloured.

3 Remove the pan from the heat and stir in the cornflour.

4 Return the pan to the heat and pour in the single cream and sherry. Simmer, stirring constantly, until thickened and smooth.

5 Add the chopped tarragon and tomato and season to taste.

6 Transfer the trout fillets to 4 individual serving plates and spoon the sauce over them. Serve immediately with buttered new potatoes and runner beans.

Trout Wrapped in a Blanket

The 'blanket' of streaky bacon bastes the fish during cooking, keeping it moist and adding flavour at the same time.

INGREDIENTS

Serves 4

juice of ½ lemon

4 trout, about 275g/10oz each

4 thyme sprigs

8 thin slices streaky bacon, rinds removed

salt and freshly ground black pepper

chopped fresh parsley and thyme sprigs,
   to garnish

lemon wedges, to serve

1 Squeeze lemon juice over the skin and in the cavity of each fish, season all over, then put a thyme sprig in each cavity.

2 Stretch each bacon slice using the back of a knife, then wind 2 slices around each fish. Preheat the oven to 200°C/400°F/Gas 6.

3 Place the fish in a lightly greased, shallow baking dish with the loose ends of bacon tucked underneath to prevent them unwinding.

4 Bake in the preheated oven for about 15–20 minutes, until the trout flesh flakes easily when tested with the point of a sharp knife and the bacon is crisp and is just beginning to brown.

5 To serve, sprinkle the trout with chopped parsley, then garnish with sprigs of thyme and accompany with lemon wedges.

COOK'S TIP

You can partially prepare this dish in advance. The trout can be wrapped in bacon and kept, covered, in the refrigerator until you are ready to cook. Return them to room temperature about 20 minutes before baking.

Salmon with Watercress Sauce

Adding the watercress right at the end of cooking retains much of its flavour and colour.

INGREDIENTS

Serves 4

300ml/½ pint/1¼ cups crème fraîche

30ml/2 tbsp chopped fresh tarragon

25g/1oz unsalted butter

15ml/1 tbsp sunflower oil

4 salmon fillets, skinned and boned

1 garlic clove, crushed

100ml/3½fl oz/scant ½ cup dry white wine

1 bunch watercress

salt and freshly ground black pepper

salad leaves, to serve

1 Gently heat the crème fraîche in a small pan until just beginning to boil. Remove the pan from the heat and stir in half the tarragon. Leave the herb cream to infuse while you cook the fish.

2 Heat the butter and oil in a frying pan, add the salmon and fry for 3–5 minutes on each side. Remove from the pan and keep warm.

3 Add the garlic to the pan and fry for 1 minute, then pour in the wine and let it bubble until reduced to about 15ml/1 tbsp.

4 Meanwhile, strip the leaves off the watercress stalks and chop finely. Discard any damaged leaves. (Save the watercress stalks for soup, if you like.)

5 Strain the herb cream into the pan and cook for a few minutes, stirring until the sauce has thickened. Stir in the remaining chopped tarragon and the watercress, then cook for a few minutes, until wilted but still bright green. Season and serve at once, spooned over the salmon. Serve with salad leaves.

Salmon with Green Peppercorns

A fashionable discovery of nouvelle cuisine, green peppercorns add piquancy to all kinds of sauces and stews. Available pickled in jars or cans, they are great to keep on hand in your store cupboard.

INGREDIENTS

Serves 4

15g/½oz butter

2 or 3 shallots, finely chopped

15ml/1 tbsp brandy (optional)

60ml/4 tbsp white wine

90ml/6 tbsp fish or chicken stock

120ml/4fl oz/½ cup whipping cream

30–45ml/2–3 tbsp green peppercorns in
    brine, rinsed

15–30ml/1–2 tbsp vegetable oil

4 pieces salmon fillet, 175–200g/
    6–7oz each

salt and freshly ground black pepper

fresh parsley, to garnish

1 Melt the butter in a heavy-based saucepan over a medium heat. Add the shallots and cook for about 1–2 minutes, until just softened but not coloured.

2 Add the brandy, if using, and the white wine, then add the stock and bring to the boil. Boil vigorously to reduce by three-quarters, stirring occasionally.

3 Reduce the heat, then add the cream and half the pepper-corns, crushing them slightly with the back of a spoon. Cook very gently for 4–5 minutes, until the sauce is slightly thickened, then strain and stir in the remaining peppercorns. Keep the sauce warm over a very low heat, stirring occasionally, while you cook the salmon fillets.

4 In a large, heavy frying pan, heat the oil over a medium-high heat until very hot. Lightly season the salmon and cook for 3–4 minutes, until the flesh is opaque throughout. To check, pierce the fish with the tip of a sharp knife; the juices should run clear. Arrange the fish on warmed plates and pour over the sauce. Garnish with parsley and serve.

Salmon with a Tarragon Mushroom Sauce

Tarragon has a distinctive aniseed flavour that is good with fish, cream and mushrooms. This recipe uses oyster mushrooms to provide both texture and flavour.

INGREDIENTS

Serves 4

50g/2oz unsalted butter
4 x 175g/6oz salmon steaks
1 shallot, finely chopped
175g/6oz assorted wild and cultivated
  mushrooms, such as oyster
  mushrooms, saffron milk-caps, bay
  boletus or cauliflower fungus, trimmed
  and sliced
200ml/7fl oz/scant 1 cup chicken or
  vegetable stock
10ml/2 tsp cornflour
2.5ml/½ tsp mustard
50ml/2fl oz/¼ cup crème fraîche
45ml/3 tbsp chopped fresh tarragon
5ml/1 tsp white wine vinegar
salt and cayenne pepper
boiled new potatoes and green salad,
  to serve

1 Melt half the butter in a large frying pan, season the salmon and cook over a moderate heat for 8 minutes, turning once. Transfer to a plate, cover and keep warm.

2 Heat the remaining butter in the pan and gently fry the shallot to soften. Add the mushrooms and cook until the juices begin to flow. Add the stock and simmer for 2–3 minutes.

3 Mix together the cornflour and mustard and blend with 15ml/1 tbsp of water. Stir into the mushroom mixture and bring to a simmer, stirring, to thicken. Add the crème fraîche, tarragon, vinegar and salt and pepper to taste.

4 Spoon the mushrooms and sauce over each salmon steak and serve with new potatoes and a green salad.

COOK'S TIP

Fresh tarragon will bruise and darken quickly after chopping, so prepare the herb as and when you need it.

Chinese-spiced Fish Fillets

East meets West with this novel twist on a classic English dish.

INGREDIENTS

Serves 4

65g/2½oz plain flour

5ml/1 tsp Chinese five-spice powder

8 skinned fillets of fish, such as plaice or
  lemon sole, about 800g/1¾lb in total

1 egg, beaten to mix

40–50g/1½–2oz fine, fresh breadcrumbs

groundnut oil, for frying

25g/1oz butter

4 spring onions, cut diagonally into
  thin slices

350g/12oz tomatoes, seeded and diced

30ml/2 tbsp soy sauce

salt and freshly ground black pepper

chives and strips of red pepper, to garnish

1 Sift the flour together with the Chinese five-spice powder and salt and pepper to taste on to a plate. Dip the fish fillets first in the seasoned flour, then in beaten egg and finally in breadcrumbs.

2 Pour the oil into a large frying pan to a depth of 1cm/½in. Heat until it is very hot and starting to sizzle. Add the coated fillets, a few at a time, and fry for 2–3 minutes, according to the thickness of the fillets, until just cooked and golden brown on both sides. Do not crowd the pan or the temperature of the oil will drop and allow the fish to absorb too much oil.

3 Drain the fillets on kitchen paper, then transfer to plates and keep warm. Pour off all the oil from the frying pan and wipe it out with kitchen paper.

4 Melt the butter in the pan and add the spring onions and tomatoes. Stir-fry for 1 minute. Stir in the soy sauce.

5 Spoon the tomato mixture over the fish and serve at once, garnished with the chives and pepper strips.

Sole, Spinach and Mushroom Muffins

English muffins, frozen spinach and a few mushrooms form the basis of this attractive and delicious recipe. Any flat fish may be used, but sole works best of all.

INGREDIENTS

Serves 2

115g/4oz butter, plus extra for spreading

1 medium onion, finely chopped

115g/4oz chestnut mushrooms, sliced

2 fresh thyme sprigs, chopped

275g/10oz frozen leaf spinach, thawed

675g/1½lb sole or plaice fillets, skinned

2 English muffins, split

60ml/4 tbsp crème fraîche

salt and freshly ground black pepper

1 Heat 50g/2oz of the butter in a saucepan. Add the onion and sauté over a low heat until it is soft, but not coloured.

2 Add the mushrooms and thyme, cover and cook for a further 2–3 minutes. Remove the lid and increase the heat to drive off excess moisture.

3 Using the back of a large spoon, press the thawed spinach in a strainer to extract all the moisture.

4 Melt 25g/1oz of the remaining butter in a saucepan. Add the spinach and heat through. Season to taste.

5 Melt the remaining butter in a large frying pan. Season the fish with salt and pepper and sauté for 2 minutes on each side.

6 Meanwhile, lightly toast then butter the split muffins. Divide the fish fillets between the muffin halves, top each with spinach and a layer of mushrooms, then finish with a spoonful of crème fraîche. Sprinkle the muffins with a little pepper and serve immediately.

Smoked Haddock and Pasta in Parsley Sauce

A creamy and delicious pasta dish with a crunchy almond topping.

Serves 4

450g/1lb smoked haddock fillet

1 small leek or onion, sliced thickly

300ml/½ pint/1¼ cups milk

1 bouquet garni (bay leaf, thyme and
    parsley stalks)

25g/1oz margarine

25g/1oz plain flour

225g/8oz pasta shells

30ml/2 tbsp chopped fresh parsley

salt and freshly ground black pepper

15g/½oz toasted flaked almonds,
    to garnish

3 Put the margarine, flour and reserved milk into a pan. Bring to the boil and whisk constantly until smooth. Season, then add the fish and leek or onion.

4 Cook the pasta in a large pan of boiling water until tender, but still firm to the bite. Drain and stir into the sauce with the chopped parsley. Serve at once, scattered with almonds.

1 Remove all the skin and any bones from the haddock. Put into a pan with the leek or onion, milk and bouquet garni. Bring to the boil, cover and simmer gently for about 8–10 minutes, until the fish flakes easily.

2 Strain, reserving the milk for making the sauce, and discard the bouquet garni.

Pan-fried Garlic Sardines

Lightly fry a sliced clove of garlic to garnish the fish. This dish could also be made with sprats or fresh anchovies, if available.

INGREDIENTS

Serves 4

1.1kg/2½lb fresh sardines

30ml/2 tbsp olive oil

4 garlic cloves

finely grated rind of 2 lemons

30ml/2 tbsp chopped fresh parsley

salt and freshly ground black pepper

For the tomato bread

2 large ripe beefsteak tomatoes

8 slices crusty bread, toasted

1 Gut and clean the sardines thoroughly.

2 Heat the oil in a frying pan and add the garlic cloves. Cook until soft.

3 Add the sardines and fry for 4–5 minutes. Sprinkle over the lemon rind, parsley and seasoning.

4 Cut the tomatoes in half and rub them on to the toast, discarding the skins. Serve the sardines with the tomato toast.

Red Snapper with Coriander Salsa

Snapper is a firm fish with little fat and benefits from a sauce with lots of texture and flavour.

INGREDIENTS

Serves 4

4 red snapper fillets, about 175g/6oz each

25ml/1½ tbsp vegetable oil

15g/½oz butter

salt and freshly ground black pepper

For the salsa

1 bunch fresh coriander, stalks removed

250ml/8fl oz/1 cup olive oil

2 garlic cloves, chopped

2 tomatoes, seeded and chopped

30ml/2 tbsp fresh orange juice

15ml/1 tbsp sherry vinegar

coriander sprigs and orange peel,
**   to garnish**

salad, to serve (optional)

3 Rinse the fish fillets and pat dry, then sprinkle with salt and pepper on both sides. Heat the oil and butter in a large frying pan. When hot, add the fish and cook for 2–3 minutes on each side, or until opaque throughout. Cook the fish in two batches, if necessary.

4 Transfer the fillets to warmed serving plates. Top with a spoonful of salsa. Serve, garnished with coriander and orange peel and with a salad, if liked.

1 To make the salsa, place the coriander, oil and garlic in a food processor or blender. Process until almost smooth. Add the tomatoes and pulse on and off several times; the mixture should be slightly chunky.

2 Transfer the mixture to a bowl. Stir in the orange juice, vinegar and salt to taste, then set the salsa aside.

Spaghettini with Vodka and Caviar

This is an elegant, yet easy, way to serve spaghettini. In Rome it is an after-theatre favourite.

INGREDIENTS

Serves 4

60ml/4 tbsp olive oil

3 spring onions, thinly sliced

1 garlic clove, finely chopped

120ml/4fl oz/½ cup vodka

150ml/¼ pint/⅔ cup double cream

150ml/¼ pint/⅔ cup black or red caviar

400g/14oz spaghettini

salt and freshly ground black pepper

COOK'S TIP

~

The finest caviar is salted sturgeon roe. Red 'caviar' is dog salmon roe, cheaper and often saltier than sturgeon roe.

1 Heat the oil in a small frying pan. Add the spring onions and garlic, and cook gently for 4–5 minutes, until softened.

2 Add the vodka and cream, and cook over low heat for about 5–8 minutes more.

3 Remove from the heat and stir in the caviar. Season with salt and pepper, as necessary.

4 Meanwhile, cook the pasta in a large pan of rapidly boiling salted water until tender, but still firm to the bite. Drain the pasta, and toss immediately to coat with the sauce. Serve at once.

Penne with Tuna and Mozzarella

This tasty sauce is quickly made from store-cupboard ingredients, with the simple addition of fresh mozzarella and parsley. If possible, use tuna canned in olive oil.

INGREDIENTS

Serves 4

400g/14oz penne, or other short pasta

15ml/1 tbsp capers, in brine or salt

2 garlic cloves

45g/3 tbsp chopped fresh parsley

200g/7oz can of tuna, drained

75ml/5 tbsp olive oil

salt and freshly ground black pepper

115g/4oz mozzarella cheese, cut into small dice

1 Bring a pan of salted water to the boil and cook the pasta according to packet instructions.

2 Rinse the capers well in water. Chop them finely with the garlic. Combine with the parsley and the tuna. Stir in the oil, and season to taste.

3 Drain the pasta when it is just tender, but still firm to the bite. Tip it into a large frying pan. Add the tuna sauce and the diced mozzarella. Cook over moderate heat, stirring constantly, until the cheese is just beginning to melt. Serve at once.

Tagliatelle with Smoked Salmon

This is a pretty pasta sauce that tastes as good as it looks. The light texture of the cucumber perfectly complements the fish. Different effects and colour combinations can be achieved by using green, white or red tagliatelle – or even a mixture of all three.

INGREDIENTS

Serves 4

350g/12oz dried or fresh tagliatelle
½ cucumber
75g/3oz butter
grated rind of 1 orange
30ml/2 tbsp chopped fresh dill
300ml/½ pint/1¼ cups single cream
15ml/1 tbsp orange juice
115g/4oz smoked salmon, skinned
salt and freshly ground black pepper

1 If using dried pasta, cook in lightly salted boiling water following the manufacturer's instructions on the packet. If using fresh pasta, cook in lightly salted boiling water for 2–3 minutes, or until just tender but still firm to the bite.

2 Using a sharp knife, cut the cucumber in half lengthways, then using a small spoon scoop out the cucumber seeds and discard.

3 Turn the cucumber on to the flat side and slice it thinly.

4 Melt the butter in a heavy-based saucepan, add the grated orange rind and fresh dill and stir well. Add the cucumber and cook gently over a low heat for about 2 minutes, stirring from time to time.

5 Add the cream, orange juice and seasoning to taste and simmer gently for 1 minute.

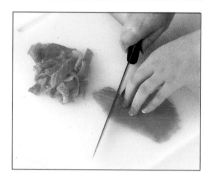

6 Meanwhile, cut the salmon into thin strips.

7 Stir the salmon into the sauce and heat through.

8 Drain the pasta thoroughly and toss it in the sauce. Serve immediately.

COOK'S TIP

A more economical way to make this special-occasion sauce is to use smoked salmon pieces, sold relatively inexpensively by most delicatessens and some super-markets. (These are just off-cuts and awkwardly shaped pieces that are unsuitable for recipes requiring whole slices of smoked salmon.) Smoked trout is a less expensive alternative, but it lacks the rich flavour and colour of smoked salmon.

Sicilian Spaghetti with Sardines

A traditional dish from Sicily, with ingredients that are common to many parts of the Mediterranean.

INGREDIENTS

Serves 4

12 fresh sardines, cleaned and boned
250ml/8fl oz/1 cup olive oil
1 onion, chopped
25g/1oz fresh dill, chopped
50g/2oz pine nuts
25g/1oz raisins, soaked in water
50g/2oz fresh breadcrumbs
450g/1lb spaghetti
flour for dusting
salt

1 Wash the sardines and pat them dry on kitchen paper. Open them out flat, then cut in half lengthways.

2 Heat 30ml/2 tbsp of the oil in a pan, add the onion and fry until golden. Add the dill and cook gently for 1–2 minutes. Add the pine nuts and raisins and season with salt to taste. Dry-fry the breadcrumbs in a frying pan until golden. Set aside.

3 Cook the spaghetti in boiling, salted water according to the instructions on the packet, until tender, but still firm to the bite. Heat the remaining oil in a pan. Dust the sardines with flour and fry in the hot oil for 2–3 minutes. Drain on kitchen paper.

4 Drain the spaghetti and return to the pan. Add the onion mixture and toss well to coat. Transfer the spaghetti mixture to a warmed serving platter and arrange the fried sardines on top. Sprinkle with the toasted bread-crumbs and serve immediately.

COOK'S TIP

Sardines are actually baby pilchards and weigh about 115g/4oz. They are covered in very fine scales and these are most easily removed with your hand, rather than with a scaling knife. Hold the fish by the tail under cold running water and rub your thumb and fingers gently along the body down to the head.

Plaice Goujons

Flat fish is ideal for making goujons. Serve with this delicious mock tartare sauce quickly made with capers, gherkins and mayonnaise.

INGREDIENTS

Serves 4

675g/1½lb plaice fillets
15ml/1 tbsp chopped fresh tarragon
175g/6oz white breadcrumbs
2 eggs, lightly beaten

For the sauce
15ml/1 tbsp capers, drained
15ml/1 tbsp gherkins, drained
150ml/¼ pint/⅔ cup mayonnaise
salt and freshly ground black pepper

1 Cut the fish fillets into strips. Preheat the oven to 220°C/ 425°F/Gas 7 and lightly grease a baking sheet.

2 In a mixing bowl, stir the tarragon and breadcrumbs together well.

3 One at a time, dip the fish strips into the egg, then in the breadcrumb mixture, coating them thoroughly. Place the fish strips on the prepared baking sheet and cook in the oven for 10 minutes.

4 Meanwhile, make the sauce. Roughly chop the capers and gherkins and stir into the mayonnaise. Season to taste with salt and pepper and serve with the crispy goujons.

Fusilli with Smoked Trout

The smoked trout and creamy sauce blend beautifully with the still crunchy vegetables.

INGREDIENTS

Serves 4–6

2 carrots, cut into julienne sticks

1 leek, cut into julienne sticks

2 sticks celery, cut into julienne sticks

150ml/¼ pint/⅔ cup vegetable stock

225g/8oz smoked trout fillets, skinned and cut into strips

200g/7oz cream cheese

150ml/¼ pint/⅔ cup medium sweet white wine or fish stock

15ml/1 tbsp chopped fresh dill or fennel

225g/8oz long curly fusilli

salt and freshly ground black pepper

dill sprigs, to garnish

1 Put the carrots, leek and celery into a pan with the vegetable stock. Bring to the boil and cook quickly for 4–5 minutes, until tender and most of the stock has evaporated. Remove from the heat and add the smoked trout.

2 To make the sauce, put the cream cheese and wine or fish stock into a saucepan, heat and whisk until smooth. Season with salt and pepper. Add the chopped dill or fennel.

3 Cook the fusilli in a pan of boiling, salted water according to the packet instructions, until tender, but firm to the bite. Drain thoroughly.

4 Return the fusilli to the pan with the sauce, toss lightly and transfer to a serving bowl. Top with the cooked vegetables and trout. Serve immediately, garnished with dill sprigs.

Farfalle with Smoked Salmon and Dill

This quick, luxurious and quite delicious sauce for pasta has now become very fashionable in Italy.

INGREDIENTS

Serves 4

6 spring onions, sliced

50g/2oz butter

90ml/6 tbsp dry white wine or vermouth

450ml/¾ pint/1⅞ cups double cream

freshly grated nutmeg

225g/8oz smoked salmon

30ml/2 tbsp chopped fresh dill

freshly squeezed lemon juice

450g/1lb farfalle (pasta bows)

salt and freshly ground black pepper

fresh dill sprigs, to garnish

1 Slice the spring onions finely. Melt the butter in a saucepan and fry the spring onions for about 1 minute, until softened.

2 Add the wine and boil hard to reduce to about 30ml/2 tbsp. Stir in the cream and add salt, pepper and nutmeg to taste. Bring to the boil and simmer for 2–3 minutes until slightly thickened.

3 Cut the smoked salmon into 2.5cm/1in squares and stir into the sauce, together with the dill. Add a little lemon juice to taste. Keep warm.

4 Cook the pasta in plenty of boiling salted water as directed. Drain well. Toss with the sauce and serve immediately, garnished with sprigs of dill.

SEAFOOD
DISHES

Noodles with Tomatoes and Prawns

Influences from Italy and the East combine in a dish with a lovely texture and taste.

INGREDIENTS

Serves 4

350g/12oz somen noodles
45ml/3 tbsp olive oil
20 raw king prawns, peeled and deveined
2 garlic cloves, finely chopped
45–60ml/3–4 tbsp sun-dried tomato paste
salt and freshly ground black pepper

For the garnish
handful of basil leaves
30ml/2 tbsp sun-dried tomatoes in oil,
   drained and cut into strips

1 Cook the noodles in a large saucepan of boiling water until tender, following the directions on the packet. Drain well.

2 Heat half the oil in a large frying pan. Add the prawns and garlic and fry them over a medium heat for 3–5 minutes, until the prawns turn pink and are firm to the touch.

3 Stir in 15ml/1 tbsp of the sun-dried tomato paste and mix well. Using a slotted spoon, transfer the prawns to a bowl and keep hot.

4 Reheat the oil remaining in the pan. Stir in the rest of the oil with the remaining sun-dried tomato paste. You may need to add a spoonful of water if the mixture is very thick.

5 When the mixture starts to sizzle, toss in the well-drained noodles. Add salt and pepper to taste and mix well.

6 Return the prawns to the pan and toss to combine. Serve at once, garnished with the basil and strips of sun-dried tomatoes.

COOK'S TIP

Ready-made sun-dried tomato paste is widely available. However, you can make your own simply by processing bottled sun-dried tomatoes with their oil. You could also add a couple of anchovy fillets and some capers if you like.

Prawns and Fish in a Herb Sauce

Bengalis are famous for their seafood dishes and always use mustard oil in recipes because it imparts a unique flavour and aroma. No feast is complete without one of these celebrated fish dishes.

INGREDIENTS

Serves 4–6

3 garlic cloves

5cm/2in piece fresh ginger

1 large leek, roughly chopped

4 green chillies

5ml/1 tsp vegetable oil (optional)

60ml/4 tbsp mustard oil

15ml/1 tbsp ground coriander

2.5ml/½ tsp fennel seeds

15ml/1 tbsp crushed yellow mustard seeds
   or 5ml/1 tsp mustard powder

175ml/6fl oz/¾ cup thick coconut milk

225g/8oz huss or monkfish, sliced

225g/8oz raw king prawns, peeled and
   deveined with tails intact

salt

115g/4oz fresh coriander leaves, chopped

green chillies, to garnish

3 Add the ground coriander, fennel seeds, mustard and coconut milk. Gently bring to the boil, then simmer, uncovered, for about 5 minutes.

4 Add the fish and simmer for 2 minutes, then fold in the prawns and cook until the prawns turn a bright orange-pink colour. Season with salt, fold in the coriander leaves and serve hot. Garnish with green chillies.

1 In a food processor, grind the garlic, ginger, leek and chillies to a coarse paste. Add vegetable oil if the mixture is too dry.

2 In a frying pan, heat the mustard oil with the paste until it is well blended. Keep the window open and take care not to overheat the mixture, as any smoke from the mustard oil will sting the eyes and irritate the nose.

Sweet and Sour Prawns

It is best to use raw prawns if available. If you are using cooked ones, add them to the sauce without the initial deep-frying.

INGREDIENTS

Serves 4–6

450g/1lb raw king prawns in their shells
vegetable oil, for deep-frying
lettuce leaves, to serve

For the sauce

15ml/1 tbsp vegetable oil
15ml/1 tbsp finely chopped spring onions
10ml/2 tsp finely chopped fresh
   root ginger
30ml/2 tbsp light soy sauce
30ml/2 tbsp soft light brown sugar
45ml/3 tbsp rice vinegar
15ml/1 tbsp Chinese rice wine or
   dry sherry
about 120ml/4fl oz/½ cup chicken or
   vegetable stock
15ml/1 tbsp cornflour paste
few drops sesame oil

1   Pull the soft legs off the prawns without removing the shells. Dry well with kitchen paper.

2   Heat the vegetable oil in a large pan or deep-fryer to 180°C/350°F and deep-fry the prawns for 35–40 seconds, or until their colour changes from grey to bright orange. Remove and drain on kitchen paper.

3   To make the sauce, heat the oil in a preheated wok, add the spring onions and ginger, followed by the seasonings and stock, and bring to the boil.

4   Add the prawns to the sauce, blend well, then thicken the sauce with the cornflour paste, stirring until smooth. Sprinkle with the sesame oil. Serve on a bed of lettuce.

Green Curry of Prawns

A popular, fragrant, creamy curry that also takes very little time to prepare. It can also be made with thin strips of chicken meat.

INGREDIENTS

Serves 4–6

30ml/2 tbsp vegetable oil

30ml/2 tbsp green curry paste

450g/1lb raw king prawns, peeled and deveined

4 kaffir lime leaves, torn

1 lemon grass stalk, bruised and chopped

250ml/8fl oz/1 cup coconut milk

30ml/2 tbsp fish sauce

½ cucumber, seeded and cut into thin batons

10–15 basil leaves

4 green chillies, sliced, to garnish

1 Heat the oil in a frying pan. Add the green curry paste and fry until bubbling and fragrant.

2 Add the prawns, kaffir lime leaves and lemon grass. Fry for 1–2 minutes, until the prawns have just turned pink.

3 Stir in the coconut milk and bring to a gentle boil. Simmer, stirring occasionally, for about 5 minutes, or until the prawns are tender. Do not overcook them.

4 Stir in the fish sauce, cucumber and basil, then top with the green chillies and serve.

Crumb-coated Prawns

Serve these crunchy breaded prawns with a home-made or ready-made dipping sauce of your choice.

INGREDIENTS

Serves 4

90g/3½oz polenta

about 5–10ml/1–2 tsp cayenne pepper

2.5ml/½ tsp ground cumin

5ml/1 tsp salt

30ml/2 tbsp chopped fresh coriander
  or parsley

1kg/2¼lb large raw prawns, peeled
  and deveined

plain flour, for dredging

50ml/2fl oz/¼ cup vegetable oil

115g/4oz coarsely grated Cheddar cheese

lime wedges and tomato salsa or relish,
  to serve

1 Mix the polenta, cayenne pepper, cumin, salt and coriander or parsley in a bowl.

2 Coat the prawns lightly in flour, then dip them in water and roll in the polenta mixture to coat evenly.

3 Heat the oil in a frying pan. When hot, add the prawns, in batches if necessary. Cook for 2–3 minutes on each side, until they are cooked through. Drain on kitchen paper.

4 Preheat the grill. Place the prawns in a baking dish or in 4 individual flameproof dishes. Sprinkle over the cheese. Grill for 2–3 minutes. Serve with lime wedges and tomato salsa or relish.

Prawn Curry with Quails' Eggs

Quails' eggs are available from speciality shops and delicatessens. Hens' eggs may be substituted if quails' eggs are hard to find. Use 1 hen's egg to every 4 quails' eggs.

INGREDIENTS

Serves 4

12 quails' eggs

30ml/2 tbsp vegetable oil

4 shallots or 1 medium onion,
   finely chopped

2.5cm/1in piece galingal or fresh root
   ginger, chopped

2 garlic cloves, crushed

5cm/2in piece lemon grass,
   finely shredded

1–2 small, fresh red chillies, seeded and
   finely chopped

2.5ml/½ tsp turmeric

1cm/½ in square piece shrimp paste or
   15ml/1 tbsp fish sauce

900g/2lb raw prawn tails, peeled
   and deveined

400ml/14fl oz/1⅔ cups canned
   coconut milk

300ml/½ pint/1¼ cups chicken stock

115g/4oz Chinese leaves,
   roughly shredded

10ml/2 tsp sugar

2.5ml/½ tsp salt

2 spring onions, green part only,
   shredded, and 30ml/2 tbsp shredded
   coconut, to garnish

1 Cook the quails' eggs in boiling water for 8 minutes. Refresh in cold water, peel and then set aside.

2 Heat the vegetable oil in a large wok, add the shallots or onion, galingal or ginger and garlic and soften without colouring. Add the lemon grass, chillies, turmeric and shrimp paste or fish sauce and fry briefly to bring out their flavours.

3 Add the prawns and fry briefly. Pour the coconut milk through a strainer over a bowl, then add the thin part of the milk with the chicken stock. Add the Chinese leaves, sugar and salt and bring to the boil. Simmer for 6–8 minutes.

4 Turn out on to a serving dish, halve the quails' eggs and toss in the sauce. Scatter with the spring onions and the shredded coconut and serve.

Indonesian Pork and Prawn Rice

Nasi Goreng is an attractive way of using up leftovers and appears in many variations throughout Indonesia. Rice is the main ingredient, although almost anything can be added for colour and flavour.

INGREDIENTS

Serves 4–6

3 eggs

60ml/4 tbsp vegetable oil

6 shallots, or 1 large onion, chopped

2 garlic cloves, crushed

2.5cm/1in piece fresh root
    ginger, chopped

2–3 small red chillies, seeded and
    finely chopped

15ml/1 tbsp tamarind sauce

1cm/½in square piece shrimp paste or
    15ml/1 tbsp fish sauce

2.5ml/½ tsp turmeric

30ml/2 tbsp unsweetened cream of coconut

juice of 2 limes

10ml/2 tsp sugar

350g/12oz lean pork or chicken breasts,
    skinned and sliced

350g/12oz raw or cooked prawn
    tails, peeled

175g/6oz bean sprouts

175g/6oz Chinese leaves, shredded

175g/6oz frozen peas, thawed

250g/9oz long grain rice, cooked

salt

1 small bunch coriander or basil, roughly
    chopped, to garnish

1 In a bowl, beat the eggs with a pinch of salt. Heat a non-stick frying pan over a moderate heat. Pour in the eggs and move the pan around until they begin to set. When set, roll up, slice thinly, cover and set aside.

2 Heat 15ml/1 tbsp of the oil in a preheated wok and fry the shallots or onion until evenly browned. Remove from the wok, set aside and keep warm.

3 Heat the remaining 45ml/ 3 tbsp of oil in the wok, add the garlic, ginger and chillies, and soften without colouring. Stir in the tamarind and shrimp paste or fish sauce, turmeric, cream of coconut, lime juice, sugar and salt to taste. Cook briefly over a moderate heat, stirring constantly. Add the pork or chicken and prawns and fry for 3–4 minutes.

4 Toss the bean sprouts, Chinese leaves and peas in the spice mixture and cook briefly. Add the rice and stir-fry for 6–8 minutes, stirring to prevent it from burning. Transfer to a large serving plate, decorate with shredded egg pancake, the fried shallots or onion, and chopped coriander or basil.

Steamed Chilli Mussels

You can add extra red chillies if you really enjoy spicy food.

Serves 6

2 fresh red chillies

6 ripe tomatoes

30ml/2 tbsp peanut oil

2 garlic cloves, crushed

2 shallots, finely chopped

1.1kg/2½lb fresh mussels

30ml/2 tbsp white wine

30ml/2 tbsp chopped fresh parsley,
    to garnish

French bread, to serve

1 Seed and roughly chop the fresh chillies. Roughly chop the tomatoes.

2 Heat the oil in a large, heavy-based saucepan and sauté the garlic and shallots over a low heat until soft and translucent.

3 Stir in the chillies and tomatoes and simmer for 10 minutes.

4 Meanwhile, debeard and scrub the mussels. Discard any that do not close when sharply tapped with the back of a knife.

5 Add the mussels and wine to the pan, cover and cook for 5 minutes, until the mussels have opened. Discard any that remain closed. Scatter over the parsley and serve with French bread.

Spicy Squid

This aromatically spiced squid dish, Cumi Cumi Smoor, is a favourite in Madura, Indonesia and is simple yet utterly delicious. Gone are the days when cleaning squid was such a chore: now they can be bought ready-cleaned and are available from fish shops, market stalls or from the freezer or fish counters of large supermarkets.

INGREDIENTS

Serves 3–4

675g/1½lb squid, cleaned

45ml/3 tbsp groundnut oil

1 onion, finely chopped

2 garlic cloves, crushed

1 beefsteak tomato, skinned and chopped

15ml/1 tbsp dark soy sauce

2.5ml/½ tsp ground nutmeg

6 cloves

150ml/¼ pint/⅔ cup water

juice of ½ lemon or lime

salt and freshly ground black pepper

boiled rice, to serve

1 Cut the squid bodies into ribbons and chop the tentacles. Rinse and drain well.

2 Heat a wok, toss in the squid and stir constantly for 2–3 minutes, by which time the squid will have curled into attractive shapes or firm rings. Lift out and set aside in a warm place.

3 Heat the oil in a clean pan and fry the onion and garlic, until soft and beginning to brown. Add the tomato, soy sauce, nutmeg, cloves, water and lemon or lime juice. Bring to the boil, then reduce the heat and add the squid with seasoning to taste.

4 Cook gently for a further 3–5 minutes, stirring from time to time. Take care not to overcook the squid. Serve hot or warm, with boiled rice.

VARIATION

Try using 450g/1lb cooked, peeled tiger prawns in this recipe. Add them for the final 1–2 minutes.

Farfalle with Prawns

Creamy sauces are not invariably the best way to serve fish with pasta. This simple, fresh prawn sauce allows the distinctive flavour of the fish to be identified.

INGREDIENTS

Serves 4

225g/8oz fresh or dried farfalle
  (pasta bows)
350g/12oz raw or cooked prawns
115g/4oz unsalted butter
2 garlic cloves, crushed
45ml/3 tbsp chopped fresh parsley
salt and freshly ground black pepper

1 If using fresh pasta, cook in boiling, salted water for 2–3 minutes, or until tender but still firm to the bite. Cook dried pasta according to the packet instructions. Peel and devein the prawns.

2 Heat the butter in a large, heavy-based saucepan with the garlic and parsley. Toss in the prawns and sauté for 8 minutes (for cooked prawns 4 minutes will be sufficient).

3 Drain the pasta thoroughly and rinse with boiling water to remove any starch.

4 Stir the pasta into the prawn mixture. Season with salt and pepper to taste and serve.

Tagliatelle with Saffron Mussels

Mussels in a saffron and cream sauce are served with tagliatelle in this recipe, but you can use any other pasta, as you prefer.

INGREDIENTS

Serves 4

1.75kg/4–4½lb mussels

150ml/¼ pint/⅔ cup dry white wine

2 shallots, chopped

350g/12oz dried tagliatelle

25g/1oz butter

2 garlic cloves, crushed

250ml/8fl oz/1 cup double cream

generous pinch of saffron strands, soaked
   in 30ml/2 tbsp hot water

1 egg yolk

salt and freshly ground black pepper

30ml/2 tbsp chopped fresh parsley,
   to garnish

1 Scrub the mussels under cold running water. Remove the beards. Discard any mussels with damaged shells or that do not shut immediately when sharply tapped.

2 Place the mussels in a large pan with the wine and shallots. Cover and cook over a high heat, shaking the pan occasionally, for 5–8 minutes, until the mussels have opened. Drain the mussels, reserving the liquid. Discard any that remain closed. Shell all but a few of the mussels and keep warm.

3 Bring the reserved cooking liquid to the boil, then boil vigorously to reduce by about half. Strain through a fine sieve into a jug to remove any grit.

4 Cook the tagliatelle in a pan of boiling salted water, according to the packet instructions, until tender, but still firm to the bite.

5 Melt the butter in a pan and fry the garlic for 1 minute. Add the mussel liquid, cream and saffron. Heat gently until the sauce thickens slightly. Remove from the heat and stir in the egg yolk, shelled mussels and seasoning.

6 Drain the pasta and transfer to serving bowls. Spoon over the sauce and sprinkle with chopped parsley. Garnish with the mussels in shells and serve at once.

Linguine with Clams

Toss together this sauce for a real seafood flavour and serve with a light mixed salad. Canned clams make this a speedy sauce for those in a real hurry.

INGREDIENTS

Serves 4

350g/12oz linguine (thin noodles)
25g/1oz butter
2 leeks, thinly sliced
150ml/¼ pint/⅔ cup dry white wine
4 tomatoes, skinned, seeded and chopped
pinch of ground turmeric (optional)
250g/9oz can clams, drained
30ml/2 tbsp chopped fresh basil
60ml/4 tbsp crème fraîche
salt and freshly ground black pepper

1 Cook the pasta following the instructions on the packet.

2 Meanwhile, melt the butter in a small saucepan and fry the leeks for about 5 minutes until softened, but not coloured.

3 Add the wine, tomatoes and turmeric, if using, bring to the boil and boil until reduced by half.

4 Stir in the clams, basil, crème fraîche and seasoning to taste and heat through gently without allowing the sauce to boil.

5 Drain the pasta thoroughly and toss it in the sauce to coat. Serve immediately.

Macaroni with King Prawns and Ham

This quick-and-easy recipe is an ideal lunch or supper dish.

INGREDIENTS

Serves 4

350g/12oz short macaroni
45ml/3 tbsp olive oil
12 raw king prawns, peeled and deveined
1 garlic clove, chopped
175g/6oz smoked ham, diced
150ml/¼ pint/⅔ cup red wine
½ small radicchio lettuce, shredded
2 egg yolks, beaten
30ml/2 tbsp chopped fresh flat leaf parsley
150ml/¼ pint/⅔ cup double cream
salt and freshly ground black pepper
shredded fresh basil, to garnish

1 Cook the pasta following the instructions on the packet.

2 Meanwhile, heat the oil in a frying pan and cook the prawns, garlic and ham for about 5 minutes, stirring occasionally, until the prawns are tender.

3 Add the wine and radicchio, bring to the boil and boil rapidly until the juices are reduced by about half.

4 Stir in the egg yolks, parsley and cream and bring almost to the boil, stirring constantly, then simmer until the sauce thickens slightly. Season to taste.

5 Drain the pasta thoroughly and toss it in the sauce to coat. Serve immediately, garnished with shredded fresh basil.

COOK'S TIP

Flat leaf parsley has more flavour than the curly variety. Finely chop any leftover parsley and freeze it in a small plastic bag. It is then ready to use for cooking, but not garnishing.

Pasta with Scallops in Green Sauce

The striking colours of this dish make it irresistible.

INGREDIENTS

Serves 4

120ml/4fl oz/½ cup low-fat crème fraîche

10ml/2 tsp wholegrain mustard

2 garlic cloves, crushed

30–45ml/2–3 tbsp fresh lime juice

60ml/4 tbsp chopped fresh parsley

30ml/2 tbsp snipped chives

350g/12oz black tagliatelle

12 large, prepared scallops

60ml/4 tbsp white wine

150ml/¼ pint/⅔ cup fish stock

salt and freshly ground black pepper

lime wedges and parsley sprigs, to garnish

1 To make the green sauce, mix the crème fraîche, mustard, garlic, lime juice, herbs and seasoning together in a bowl.

2 Cook the pasta in boiling, salted water according to the packet instructions. Drain well.

3 Slice the scallops in half, horizontally. Keep any coral whole. Put the wine and fish stock into a saucepan. Heat to simmering point. Add the scallops and cook very gently for 3–4 minutes.

4 Remove the scallops. Boil the wine and stock vigorously to reduce by half and add the green sauce to the pan. Heat gently to warm, replace the scallops and cook for 1 minute. Spoon over the pasta and garnish with lime wedges and parsley.

Seafood Spaghetti

This pasta sauce provides a truly Mediterranean flavour. Serve with thick slices of fresh Italian bread.

INGREDIENTS

Serves 4

15ml/1 tbsp olive oil

350g/12oz dried spaghetti

50g/2oz butter

1 onion, chopped

1 red pepper, seeded and coarsely chopped

2 garlic cloves, chopped

15ml/1 tbsp paprika

450g/1lb fresh mussels

150ml/¼ pint/⅔ cup dry white wine

30ml/2tbsp chopped fresh parsley

225g/8oz peeled, cooked prawns

150ml/¼ pint/⅔ cup crème fraîche

salt and freshly ground black pepper

finely chopped fresh flat leaf parsley, to garnish

Italian bread, to serve

1 Bring a large saucepan of lightly salted water to the boil. Add the olive oil and spaghetti. Bring back to the boil, lower the heat and cook for 8–10 minutes, until the spaghetti is tender, but still firm to the bite.

2 Meanwhile, melt the butter in a pan and fry the onion, pepper, garlic and paprika for 5 minutes.

3 Debeard and scrub the mussels. Discard any that do not close immediately when tapped with the back of a knife.

4 Add the wine to the pan and bring to the boil.

5 Stir in the mussels, parsley and prawns, cover and simmer for about 5 minutes, until the mussels have opened. Discard any that remain closed.

6 Remove the shellfish from the pan with a slotted spoon and keep warm. Bring the cooking juices back to the boil and boil rapidly until reduced by half.

7 Stir in the crème fraîche and blend thoroughly. Return the shellfish to the pan and simmer over a low heat for 1 minute to heat through. Taste and season.

8 Drain the spaghetti thoroughly and divide it between 4 individual serving plates. Spoon the shellfish and sauce over the top and toss, using two forks. Garnish with the chopped flat leaf parsley and serve immediately with the Italian bread.

SALADS

Warm Fish Salad with Mango Dressing

This salad is best served during the summer months, preferably out of doors. The dressing combines the flavour of rich mango with hot chilli, ginger and lime.

INGREDIENTS

Serves 4

1 French loaf

4 redfish, black bream or porgy, each weighing about 275g/10oz

15ml/1 tbsp vegetable oil

1 mango

1cm/½in fresh root ginger

1 fresh red chilli, seeded and finely chopped

30ml/2 tbsp lime juice

30ml/2 tbsp chopped fresh coriander

175g/6oz young spinach

150g/5oz pak choi

175g/6oz cherry tomatoes, halved

1 Cut the French loaf into 20cm/8in lengths. Slice lengthways, then cut into thick fingers. Place the bread on a baking sheet and dry in a preheated oven at 180°C/350°F/Gas 4 for 15 minutes. Slash the fish deeply on both sides with a sharp knife and moisten with oil. Cook under a preheated grill or on a barbecue for 6 minutes, turning once.

2 Peel and stone the mango. Slice the flesh and place half of it in a food processor. Peel and finely grate the ginger, then add to the food processor with the chilli, lime juice and coriander. Process until smooth. Adjust to a pouring consistency with 30–45ml/ 2–3 tbsp water.

3 Wash the salad leaves and spin dry, then divide them equally between 4 serving plates. Place the fish on the leaves. Spoon over the mango dressing and finish with slices of mango and cherry tomato halves. Serve with fingers of crispy French bread.

COOK'S TIP

Other fish suitable for this salad include salmon, monkfish, tuna, sea bass and halibut. Use fillets, cutlets or steaks.

Spinach Salad with Bacon and Prawns

Serve this hot salad with plenty of crusty bread for mopping up the delicious juices.

INGREDIENTS

Serves 4

105ml/7 tbsp olive oil

30ml/2 tbsp sherry vinegar

2 garlic cloves, finely chopped

5ml/1 tsp Dijon mustard

12 cooked king prawns

115g/4oz streaky bacon, rinded and cut
  into strips

about 115g/4oz fresh young
  spinach leaves

½ head oak leaf lettuce, roughly torn

salt and freshly ground black pepper

1 To make the dressing, whisk together 90ml/6 tbsp of the olive oil with the vinegar, garlic, mustard and seasoning in a small pan. Heat gently until thickened slightly, then keep warm.

2 Carefully peel the prawns, leaving the tails intact. Set aside.

3 Heat the remaining oil in a frying pan and fry the bacon until golden and crisp, stirring occasionally. Add the prawns and stir-fry for a few minutes until warmed through.

4 While the bacon and prawns are cooking, arrange the spinach and torn oak leaf lettuce leaves on four individual serving plates.

5 Spoon the bacon and prawns on to the leaves, then pour over the hot dressing. Serve at once.

COOK'S TIP

Sherry vinegar lends its pungent flavour to this delicious salad. You can buy it from most large supermarkets and delicatessens.

Salmon and Tuna Parcels

You will need fairly large smoked salmon slices as they are wrapped around a light tuna mixture before being served on a vibrant salad. Kiwi fruit is a particularly rich source of vitamin C.

INGREDIENTS

Serves 4

30ml/2 tbsp low-fat natural yogurt

15ml/1 tbsp sun-dried tomato paste

5ml/1 tsp whole grain honey mustard

grated rind and juice of 1 lime

200g/7oz can tuna in brine, drained

130g/4½oz smoked salmon slices

salt and freshly ground black pepper

fresh mint leaves, to garnish

For the salad

3 tomatoes, sliced

2 kiwi fruit, peeled and sliced

¼ cucumber, cut into julienne sticks

For the mint vinaigrette

15ml/1 tbsp wine vinegar

45ml/3 tbsp olive oil

15ml/1 tbsp chopped fresh mint

COOK'S TIP

Although healthy eating guidelines recommend reducing the amount of fat, particularly saturated fat, in the diet, salad dressings made with polyunsaturated or monounsaturated oil, such as olive oil, can and should be included, in sensible moderation. This recipe is not high in calories, but if weight control is a real issue, use an oil-free dressing instead of vinaigrette.

1 Mix the yogurt, tomato paste and mustard in a bowl. Stir in the grated lime rind and juice. Add the tuna, with black pepper to taste, and mix well.

2 Spread out the salmon slices on a board and spoon some of the tuna mixture on to each piece.

3 Roll up or fold the smoked salmon into neat parcels. Carefully press the edges together to seal.

4 Make the salad. Arrange the tomato and kiwi slices on 4 serving plates. Scatter over the cucumber sticks.

5 Make the vinaigrette. Put all the ingredients in a screw-top jar, season with salt and pepper and shake vigorously. Spoon a little vinaigrette over each salad.

6 Arrange 3–4 salmon parcels on each salad, garnish with the mint leaves and serve.

Warm Salmon Salad

Light and fresh, this salad is perfect for an al fresco summer lunch. Serve it immediately, or you'll find the salad leaves will lose their bright colour and texture.

INGREDIENTS

Serves 4

450g/1lb salmon fillet, skinned

30ml/2 tbsp sesame oil

grated rind of ½ orange

juice of 1 orange

5ml/1 tsp Dijon mustard

15ml/1 tbsp chopped fresh tarragon

45ml/3 tbsp groundnut oil

115g/4oz fine green beans, trimmed

175g/6oz mixed salad leaves, such as
    young spinach leaves, radicchio, frisée
    and oak leaf lettuce leaves

15ml/1 tbsp toasted sesame seeds

salt and freshly ground black pepper

1 Cut the salmon into bite-sized pieces, then make the dressing. Mix together the sesame oil, orange rind and juice, mustard, chopped tarragon and seasoning in a bowl. Set aside.

2 Heat the groundnut oil in a frying pan. Add the salmon pieces and fry for 3–4 minutes, until lightly browned but still tender inside.

3 Meanwhile, blanch the green beans in boiling salted water for about 5–6 minutes, until they are tender, but still crisp.

4 Add the dressing to the salmon, toss together gently and cook for 30 seconds. Remove the pan from the heat.

5 Arrange the salad leaves on 4 serving plates. Drain the beans and toss over the leaves. Spoon over the salmon and cooking juices and serve immediately, sprinkled with the sesame seeds.

Melon and Crab Salad

*A perfect summer salad when crab
and melon are in generous supply.*

Serves 6

450g/1lb fresh cooked crab meat
120ml/4fl oz/½ cup mayonnaise
45ml/3 tbsp soured cream or
   natural yogurt
30ml/2 tbsp olive oil
30ml/2 tbsp fresh lemon or lime juice
2–3 spring onions, finely chopped
30ml/2 tbsp finely chopped
   fresh coriander
1.5ml/¼ tsp cayenne pepper
1½ cantaloupe or small honeydew melons
3 medium chicory heads
salt and freshly ground black pepper
fresh coriander sprigs, to garnish

1 Pick over the crab meat very carefully, removing any bits of shell or cartilage. Leave the pieces of crab meat as large as possible.

2 In a medium-sized bowl, combine mayonnaise, soured cream or yogurt, olive oil, lemon or lime juice, spring onions, chopped coriander and cayenne pepper and season to taste with salt and pepper. Mix well, then fold the crab meat into this dressing.

3 Halve the melons and remove and discard the seeds. Cut the melons into thin slices, then remove the rind.

4 Divide the salad between 6 individual serving plates, making a decorative design with the melon slices and whole chicory leaves. Place a mound of dressed crab meat on each plate and garnish the salads with one or two fresh coriander sprigs.

Mediterranean Salad with Basil

A type of Salade Niçoise with pasta, this conjures up all the sunny flavours of the Mediterranean.

Serves 4

225g/8oz chunky pasta shapes

175g/6oz fine green beans

2 large ripe tomatoes

50g/2oz fresh basil leaves

200g/7oz can tuna fish in oil, drained and roughly flaked

2 hard-boiled eggs, shelled and sliced or quartered

50g/2oz can anchovy fillets, drained

salt and freshly ground black pepper

capers and black olives, to garnish

For the dressing

90ml/6 tbsp extra virgin olive oil

30ml/2 tbsp white wine vinegar or lemon juice

2 garlic cloves, crushed

2.5ml/½ tsp Dijon mustard

30ml/2 tbsp chopped fresh basil

1 Whisk all the ingredients for the dressing together, season with salt and pepper and leave to infuse while you make the salad.

2 Cook the pasta in plenty of boiling, salted water according to the manufacturer's instructions. Drain well and set aside to cool.

3 Trim the green beans and blanch them in boiling salted water for 3 minutes. Drain, then refresh in cold water.

4 Slice or quarter the tomatoes and arrange on the base of a bowl. Moisten with a little dressing and cover with a quarter of the basil leaves. Then cover with the beans. Moisten with a little more dressing and cover with a third of the remaining basil.

5 Cover with the pasta tossed in a little more dressing, half the remaining basil and the roughly flaked tuna.

6 Arrange the eggs on top. Finally, scatter over the anchovy fillets, capers and black olives. Pour over the remaining dressing and garnish with the remaining basil. Serve at once. Do not be tempted to chill this salad – all the flavour will be dulled.

COOK'S TIP

Olives marinated in oil flavoured with garlic, herbs and lemon peel would add an extra-special touch to this salad. Choose plump, black olives that are fully ripened. Marinated olives are available from large supermarkets and delicatessens or you could prepare them yourself.

Avocado and Smoked Fish Salad

*Avocado and smoked fish make an
excellent combination, and
flavoured with herbs and spices,
create a delectable salad.*

INGREDIENTS

Serves 4

15g/½oz butter or margarine

½ onion, finely sliced

5ml/1 tsp mustard seeds

225g/8oz smoked mackerel, flaked

30ml/2 tbsp chopped, fresh coriander

2 firm tomatoes, skinned and chopped

15ml/1 tbsp lemon juice

salt and freshly ground black pepper

For the salad

2 avocado pears

½ cucumber

15ml/1 tbsp lemon juice

2 firm tomatoes

1 green chilli

1 Melt the butter or margarine
in a frying pan, add the onion
and mustard seeds and fry for
about 5 minutes, until the onion is
soft, but not coloured.

2 Add the fish, coriander leaves,
tomatoes and lemon juice and
cook over a low heat for 2–3
minutes. Remove from the heat
and set aside to cool.

3 Make the salad. Peel and thinly
slice the avocado pears and
slice the cucumber. Put into a bowl
and sprinkle with the lemon juice.

4 Slice the tomatoes. Seed and
finely chop the chilli.

5 Place the fish mixture in the
centre of a serving plate.

6 Arrange the avocado pears,
cucumber and tomatoes
around the fish. Alternatively,
spoon a quarter of the fish mixture
on to each of 4 serving plates and
divide the avocados, cucumber and
tomatoes equally. Sprinkle with the
chopped chilli and a little salt and
pepper and serve.

Tuna and Bean Salad

*This substantial salad makes a good
light meal and can be assembled
from canned ingredients quickly.*

INGREDIENTS

Serves 4–6

2 x 400g/14oz cans cannellini or
    borlotti beans
2 x 200g/7oz cans tuna fish, drained
60ml/4 tbsp extra virgin olive oil
30ml/2 tbsp fresh lemon juice
15ml/1 tbsp chopped fresh parsley
3 spring onions, thinly sliced
salt and freshly ground black pepper

1 Pour the beans into a large
strainer and rinse under cold
water. Drain well. Place in a
serving dish.

2 Break the tuna into fairly large
flakes and arrange over the
beans in the serving dish.

3 In a small bowl make the
dressing by combining the oil
with the lemon juice. Season with
salt and pepper and stir in the
parsley. Mix well. Pour over the
beans and tuna.

4 Sprinkle with the spring
onions. Toss the salad well
before serving.

Thai Seafood Salad

This unusual seafood salad with chilli, lemon grass and fish sauce is light and refreshing.

INGREDIENTS

Serves 4

225g/8oz ready-prepared squid

225g/8oz raw tiger prawns

8 scallops, shelled

225g/8oz firm white fish

30–45ml/2–3 tbsp olive oil

small mixed lettuce leaves and coriander
    sprigs, to serve

For the dressing

2 small fresh red chillies, seeded and
    finely chopped

5cm/2in piece lemon grass, finely chopped

2 fresh kaffir lime leaves, shredded

30ml/2 tbsp Thai fish sauce (*nam pla*)

2 shallots, thinly sliced

30ml/2 tbsp lime juice

30ml/2 tbsp rice vinegar

10ml/2 tsp caster sugar

1 Prepare the seafood. Slit open the squid bodies, cut into square pieces, then score the flesh in a criss-cross pattern with a sharp knife. Halve the tentacles, if necessary. Peel and devein the prawns. Remove the dark beard-like fringe and tough muscle from the scallops. Cube the white fish.

2 Heat a wok or large frying pan until hot. Add the oil and swirl it around, then add the prawns and stir-fry for 2–3 minutes until pink. Transfer to a large bowl. Stir-fry the squid and scallops for 1–2 minutes until opaque. Remove and add to the prawns. Stir-fry the white fish for 2–3 minutes. Remove and add to the cooked seafood. Reserve any juices.

3 Put all the dressing ingredients in a small bowl with the reserved juices from the wok or frying pan and mix well.

4 Pour the dressing over the seafood and toss gently. Arrange the salad leaves and coriander sprigs on 4 individual plates, then spoon the seafood on top. Serve at once.

Aubergine Salad with Dried Shrimps

An appetizing and unusual salad that you will find yourself making over and over again.

Serves 4–6

2 aubergines

15ml/1 tbsp oil

30ml/2 tbsp dried shrimps, soaked
    and drained

15ml/1 tbsp coarsely chopped garlic

30ml/2 tbsp freshly squeezed lime juice

5ml/1 tsp palm or brown sugar

30ml/2 tbsp fish sauce

1 hard-boiled egg, shelled and chopped

4 shallots, finely sliced into rings

coriander leaves and 2 red chillies, seeded
    and sliced, to garnish

1 Grill or roast the aubergines until charred and tender.

2 When the aubergines are cool enough to handle, peel away the skin and slice the flesh.

3 Heat the oil in a small frying pan, add the drained shrimps and garlic and fry for 3–4 minutes, until golden. Remove from the pan and set aside.

4 To make the dressing, put the lime juice, palm or brown sugar and fish sauce in a small bowl and whisk together.

5 To serve, arrange the aubergines on a serving dish. Top with the egg, shallots and dried shrimp mixture. Drizzle over the dressing and garnish with coriander and chillies.

COOK'S TIP
~
For an interesting variation, try using salted ducks' or quails' eggs, cut in half, instead of chopped hens' eggs.

Seafood Salad with Fragrant Herbs

This tasty medley of seafood and noodles is a meal in itself.

INGREDIENTS

Serves 4–6

250ml/8fl oz/1 cup fish stock or water

350g/12oz squid, cleaned and cut into rings

12 raw king prawns, peeled and deveined

12 scallops, cleaned

50g/2oz bean thread noodles, soaked in
    warm water for 30 minutes

½ cucumber, cut into thin sticks

1 stalk lemon grass, finely chopped

2 kaffir lime leaves, finely shredded

2 shallots, finely sliced

juice of 1–2 limes

30ml/2 tbsp fish sauce

30ml/2 tbsp chopped spring onion

30ml/2 tbsp coriander leaves

12–15 mint leaves, roughly torn

4 red chillies, seeded and sliced

coriander sprigs, to garnish

1 Pour the fish stock or water into a medium-size saucepan, set over a high heat and bring to the boil.

2 Place each type of seafood individually in the stock and cook for a few minutes. Remove and set aside.

3 Drain the bean thread noodles and cut them into short lengths, about 5cm/2in long. Combine the noodles with the cooked seafood.

4 Add the cucumber, lemon grass, kaffir lime leaves, shallots, lime juice, fish sauce, spring onion, coriander and mint leaves and chillies and mix together well. Serve garnished with the coriander sprigs.

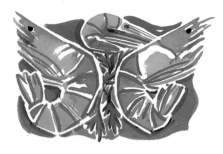

Pomelo Salad

Pomelo is a large, pear-shaped fruit that resembles a grapefruit.

INGREDIENTS

Serves 4-6

30ml/2 tbsp vegetable oil

4 shallots, finely sliced

2 garlic cloves, finely sliced

1 large pomelo

15ml/1 tbsp roasted peanuts

115g/4oz cooked peeled prawns

115g/4oz cooked crab meat

10–12 small mint leaves

2 spring onions, finely sliced

2 red chillies, seeded and finely sliced

coriander leaves, to garnish

shredded fresh coconut (optional)

For the dressing

30ml/2 tbsp fish sauce

15ml/1 tbsp palm or brown sugar

30ml/2 tbsp lime juice

1 Make the dressing. Whisk together the fish sauce, palm or brown sugar and lime juice and set aside.

2 Heat the oil in a small frying pan, add the shallots and garlic and fry for 3–4 minutes, until they are golden. Remove from the pan and set aside.

3 Peel the pomelo and break the flesh into small pieces, taking care to remove any membranes.

4 Coarsely grind the peanuts, then combine with the pomelo flesh, prawns, crab meat, mint leaves and the fried shallot mixture. Toss the salad in the dressing and serve sprinkled with the spring onions, red chillies, coriander leaves and shredded coconut, if using.

Prawn Salad with Curry Dressing

Curry spices add an unexpected twist to this salad. Warm flavours combine especially well with sweet prawns and grated apple.

INGREDIENTS

Serves 4

1 ripe tomato

½ iceberg lettuce, shredded

1 small onion

1 small bunch fresh coriander

15ml/1 tbsp lemon juice

450g/1lb cooked peeled prawns

1 apple, peeled

salt

8 whole cooked prawns, 8 lemon wedges
and 4 sprigs fresh coriander, to garnish

For the dressing

75ml/5 tbsp mayonnaise

5ml/1 tsp mild curry paste

15ml/1 tbsp tomato ketchup

30ml/2 tbsp water

1 To peel the tomato, pierce the skin with a knife and immerse in boiling water for 20 seconds. Drain and cool under running water. Peel off the skin. Halve the tomato, push the seeds out with your thumb and discard them. Cut the flesh into large dice.

2 Finely shred the lettuce, onion and coriander. Add the tomato, moisten with lemon juice and season with salt.

3 To make the dressing, mix together the mayonnaise, curry paste and tomato ketchup in a small bowl. Add the water to thin the dressing and season to taste with salt.

4 Combine the prawns with the dressing. Quarter and core the apple and grate into the mixture.

5 Distribute the shredded lettuce and onion mixture between 4 plates or bowls. Pile the prawn mixture in the centre of each and garnish with 2 whole prawns, 2 lemon wedges and a sprig of coriander.

COOK'S TIP

Fresh coriander is inclined to wilt if it is not kept in water. Store it in a jar of water, covered with a plastic bag, in the refrigerator and it will stay fresh for several days.

Prawn and Pasta Salad with Green Dressing

*Anchovies need a nice strong
dressing to match their flavour.*

Serves 4-6

4 anchovy fillets, drained

60ml/4 tbsp milk

225g/8oz squid

15ml/1 tbsp chopped capers

15ml/1 tbsp chopped gherkins

1–2 garlic cloves, crushed

150ml/¼ pint/⅔ cup natural yogurt

30–45ml/2–3 tbsp mayonnaise

squeeze of lemon juice

50g/2oz watercress, chopped finely

30ml/2 tbsp chopped fresh parsley

30ml/2 tbsp chopped fresh basil

350g/12oz fusilli (pasta spirals)

350g/12oz cooked peeled prawns

salt and freshly ground black pepper

1 Put the anchovies into a small bowl and cover with the milk. Leave to soak for 10 minutes. Pull the heads from the squid and remove and discard the quills. Peel the outer speckled skin from the bodies and rinse well. Cut into 5mm/¼in rings. Cut the tentacles from the heads, rinse under cold water and cut into 5mm/¼in slices.

2 To make the dressing, mix the capers, gherkins, garlic, yogurt, mayonnaise, lemon juice and fresh herbs in a bowl. Drain and chop the anchovies. Add to the dressing with the seasoning.

3 Drop the squid rings and tentacles into a large pan of boiling, salted water. Lower the heat and simmer for 1–2 minutes (do not overcook or the squid will become tough). Remove with a slotted spoon. Cook the pasta in the same water according to the instructions on the packet. Drain thoroughly.

4 Mix the prawns and squid into the dressing in a large bowl. Add the pasta, toss and serve immediately. Alternatively, allow to cool and serve as a salad.

Index